Praise for *The Mother's Guide* and for Renée Trudeau

"Parenting grows our patience and generosity. Trudeau's wise book reminds us that co[...] will keep us fit to become the most excellent loving parents we can possibly be. The *Guid[...]* to creating a more enlightened society."

—**Linda Bloom**, co-author of *101 Things I Wish I Knew When I Got Married: Simple Less[...]*

Renée Trudeau's *Guide* can literally change our world. As mothers join in small gro[...] personal growth, the positive and powerful ripple effects in the family will have far-rea[...] cross cultural norms. What this *Guide* really represents is an owner's manual for what it is to be a well-balanced human being. Buy this for your best friend, and then join her in creating your own Personal Renewal Group and watch your life flourish into what you only dreamed it could be.

—**Celeste Hamman**, coach/author and past president of the Austin Chapter of the International Coaches Federation

"This book is truly an important tool for transformation—not only for moms with newborns, but for women with children of all ages. Mothers often feel lost and alone. They need help, and this important guide shows them how to ask for and receive help in a multitude of ways."

—**Susan Jeffers**, PhD, author of *Feel the Fear and Do It Anyway* and *I'm Okay...You're a Brat!*

"Every mother needs an artery of life that pumps her self-worth outside of her spouse, children and home. Renée reminds women to keep the 'me' part of Mommy passionate, growing and alive."

—**Iris Krasnow**, best-selling author of *Surrendering to Motherhood* and *I Am My Mother's Daughter*

"*The Mother's Guide to Self-Renewal* is a must for all mothers and moms-to-be. The warm, inviting and entertaining style of this book makes it like a flowing conversation with a trusted and wise friend—someone you can count on to point you to your own knowing. Renée has wondrously created a roadmap for mothers to tap their innate capacity for wisdom, renewal and self-love. This state of mind is a mother's greatest resource for her job as a parent and her source for performing that role with joy, confidence and love."

—**Frances A. Cox**, LPC, president/owner, Southwest Center for Health Realization

"Becoming a parent is a wild and wondrous journey. For a woman, it's a crazy love with an extreme learning curve that's indescribable. One day we take a wave and it brings us to shore. We love those days. The next days we tumble madly, not knowing up from down. Doubts run amuck, and balance appears a distant memory. This bold and beautiful book will bring us home. Renée's compassion and clarity of guidance is a gift to us all."

—**Gail Allen**, internationally known parenting and leadership coach

"In our 24/7 world, all moms, whether they are home full-time with children or actively employed, need help balancing their multiple roles and responsibilities. This book is a gem—filled with inspirational wisdom and useful strategies that will help generate a greater sense of calm, control and joy in your life."

—**Nancy Collamer**, founder of Jobsandmoms.com

"*The Mother's Guide to Self-Renewal* is a powerful and life-shifting book for every mom who continuously falls to the bottom of her 'to-do' list and forgets about the things that make her happy and feel her best. This practical and life-affirming resource empowers moms to reflect, renew and rejuvenate."

—**Natalie Gahrmann**, MA, ACC coach and author of *Succeeding as a SuperBusy Parent*

"Wow, what a terrific guide for moms! Where else can we learn the stuff our mothers certainly never taught us about caring well for ourselves? Far more than fluffy 'bubble bath' ideas, Renée has gathered insightful wisdom into engaging, inspiring and easy-to-follow steps. These simple, powerful ideas will help you find joy, meaning and connection to your Self and others, even when you're knee-deep in diapers!"

—**Sharon Day**, author/coach, www.sharonday.com

"Yes, yes, yes! This is just what I've been looking for! As an early parenting coach, I work primarily with women during the transition into motherhood. Renée not only understands the challenges and needs of the 21st-century mother, she offers them a guide for self-discovery and renewal. This should be required reading for all mothers, mothers-to-be and anyone working with women during this transformative time of life."

—**Carrie Contey**, PhD, board member, Association of Pre- and Perinatal Psychology and Health

"The book was written as if Renée had read my mind and decided to write a *Guide* just for me. Finding who I am, seeking balance while juggling my many roles and identifying and staying true to my life's priorities are all areas I have explored as I approach 40. Renée has been blessed with an uncanny ability to look inward and make sense of what mothers are feeling."

—**Annemarie Kirkpatrick**, mother of five and self-employed consultant

"Renée has written the book I desperately needed when I became a mother. How I wish I had had this illuminating, encouraging and wise book to light my path in those early years. The *Guide* is a priceless gift for mothers everywhere. It is sure to enhance the lives of all mothers fortunate enough to read it, and therefore the lives of countless children as well."

—**Alyson Stone**, PhD, licensed psychologist and president of LifeBalance Inc.

"A nice reminder that happy parents make happy children!"

—**Ari Brown**, MD, co-author of *Baby 411* and *Toddler 411*

"Renée's book is a wonderful guide for all stages of motherhood. She not only reinforces the importance of self-care, she provides the tools to help mothers renew and rejuvenate when knowing where to start the process is the hardest part! I look forward to sharing this treasure with other women in my community."

—**Meg Kanewske**, prenatal/hatha yoga teacher, Yoga Yoga

"This is a fabulous guide to balanced living for mothers, or anyone for that matter. I love the month-to-month approach and the variety of ideas/exercises you offer women so they can make the themes part of their everyday life. It is great for moms to have a guide that addresses the realities and challenges associated with the wonderful journey called motherhood."

—**Karen Swenson**, MD, founding partner of Women Partners in Health and fellow, American College of Obstetricians and Gynecologists

"This book is not just for new mothers! I want to do the exercises in the book for myself, a menopausal, empty-nester, midwife! The questions and insights are valuable for any woman at any point in life—especially life junctions. As a midwife, it is easy to spend so much time on my professional demands and my clients' needs that my own needs are often supplanted. The *Guide* helps me to remember who I am and to take time for myself and that spiritual connection and community are keystones for me. This wonderful resource serves as a grounding and inspiring instruction book on life."

—**Mary Barnett**, CNM, MN, RN, president, Heart of Texas Midwives

"Parenting is the most human activity. It can be joyful but also overwhelming. Renée's insights and ideas will be a great tool for mothers navigating and experiencing the richness of this most important role."

—**Mark Levy**, MD, South Austin Medical Clinic

"You wouldn't think that a book on life balance for mothers would be a 'page-turner'—this one is. I read it in two sittings. I couldn't wait to get to the next chapter. Renée has gotten to the core of what we need in our lives—as women, as mothers and as people. She reminds us how to return to that core."

—**Margaret Keys**, nationally-known executive coach for Fortune 500 companies

"The *Guide* is an excellent self-renewal source for mothers to rediscover their own personal identity and power. It takes the concept of group interaction and sharing of thoughts, goals and feelings and creates a dynamic life plan focused on personal growth and renewal. As it 'takes a village' to raise a child you might say it takes a Personal Renewal Group to trigger personal and spiritual growth."

—**Jerry Hudson**, MD, pediatrician and founding partner, Bee Caves Pediatrics

"I LOVED the book. The content is so rich—I really feel like a different person after reading it! It was a renewing experience. You have touched so deeply on so many areas that resonate with mothers. Thank you for deeply touching my heart."

—**Carey Youngblood**, founder/president, Heartsong Music Together

"Being a mom/musician/entrepreneur requires a lot of planning and support via friends and family, the ability to say 'no' and taking time for self-care. *The Mother's Guide* strengthens and supports these essentials for hard-working moms looking for answers, and it will give new moms a roadmap for their changing lives."

—**Sara Hickman**, nationally known recording artist/creative elf

NOT FOR
RESALE

The Mother's Guide to
Self-Renewal

How to Reclaim, Rejuvenate
and Re-Balance Your Life

Renée Peterson Trudeau

BALANCED LIVING PRESS • AUSTIN TEXAS

Balanced Living Press
4107 Medical Parkway, Suite 104
Austin, TX 78756
512-459-6700

Cover and text designed by Bella Guzmán (www.bellaguzman.com)
Front and back cover photos by Anne Butler Photography (www.annebutler.com)
Mandala illustrations by Heidi Priesnitz (www.hidesigngraphics.com)

Disclaimer: The names used in some of the personal stories in the Guide
have been changed at the participants' request.

FIRST EDITION
ISBN: 978-0-9789776-0-3

This book holds in her heart all the motherless mothers—whether their loss is physical or emotional—who are learning that the most important nurturing you can receive is the love you shower upon yourself.

table of contents

The photographs in the Guide were taken by author Renée Trudeau. For the past twenty years, she has combined her passions for travel and black and white photography to create photos similar to the ones in this book.

Ancient ruins at Ephesus, Western Turkey

The Evolution of
The Mother's Guide to Self-Renewal and How to Use This Book

I believe it's your birthright to live the life you desire. This is why I created *The Mother's Guide to Self-Renewal.*

The life I desire is marked by a deep connection to my child and to my partner. It's a life filled with joy and meaning. It's a life in which I feel supported and nurtured by an incredible community of women—young and old. I experience regular, meaningful, heartfelt connections with people I care about. I am continually open to growth—as a woman, a mother, a partner and a spiritual being. I enjoy supporting and serving others in a way that feeds me rather than drains me. I feel that I always have enough time in my life for those things that are most important to me. My life flows, I trust my intuition and I expect good to come to me. I feel peaceful. I am loving, and I feel loved.

This is the life I desire.

It was only after I became a mother that I was finally able to articulate this.

When I was pregnant, I had so many unanswered questions running through my mind—probably more than at any other time in my life.

How would I feel about going back to work after the baby came? If and when I went back to work, how would I ever find a caregiver I trusted enough to watch my child? How would I find balance in the midst of all of this? How would the baby change my marriage?

As my belly expanded, I began to feel like a host for an alien (I was!). *Would I ever get my body back? What kind of parent would I be? Would becoming a mom change how I felt about myself?* The list went on and on.

Having a baby is **so** life changing; it brings up questions and insecurities many of us didn't even know we had! The only way I can describe the transition is: becoming a mother changes a woman *on a cellular level*—it truly affects how you see and feel about everything in your world.

After having my son, Jonah, in March 2002, I discovered—and experienced firsthand—a startling and disturbing truth about mothers everywhere.

I suddenly became aware of how little we cared for ourselves (especially in relation to how much energy we give our children) and how changed and disconnected most of us felt from *ourselves* after becoming parents. Whether this question of identity lasts until your child turns six months old or continues into the high school years, mothers everywhere are wondering, *Now who am I?*

I had been introduced to the powerful message of "self-care" through author/life coach Cheryl Richardson's book *Life Makeovers* in 2000, when I facilitated a *Life Makeovers* group for some friends. Some of the women in the group were mothers, while others (including me) were not.

I knew from that experience that if anyone needed to make time for self-care, it was mothers.

After Jonah turned six months old, I felt a growing sense of urgency to reach out to mothers and create a dialogue around the topic of self-care. In January 2003, I launched the first Personal Renewal Group (PRG) for mothers in Austin, Texas. The group, which was limited to twenty participants, filled immediately.

The idea behind the PRG was to create an ongoing forum for mothers to share and explore meaningful themes that weren't typical playgroup discussion topics, such as how to create life balance and reconnect with "who you are."

My experience with my own playgroups (which were very vital and nurturing to my well-being) was that conversation tended to focus on the children's physical and developmental needs. Turning to a friend in a weekly playgroup and asking, "Tell me about your personal support system" or "What in your life right now is draining you or fueling you?" is clearly not the norm; in fact, many moms might feel this type of conversation is awkward in such a setting.

Paradoxically, through my work with clients as a career coach and in my own life, I've observed that what people want most in this age of isolation is meaningful connection and community with others.

Based on this observation, I believe that one of the most effective ways to grow (personally and spiritually) and become emotionally whole is by sharing with others at similar life stages in an empowering, supportive and nurturing group setting.

In 2003, at the urging of many PRG members who wanted to share the self-renewal program and exercises with their friends throughout the U.S. and Canada, I created *The Mother's Guide to Self-Renewal*, so that women everywhere could use the *Guide* and form their own Personal

Renewal Groups in their community. (See the end of the *Guide* for more information and visit www.reneetrudeau.com to learn how to start or join a group.)

My intention for the *Guide* is that it will serve as a catalyst for your healing, growth and personal empowerment.

I have seen women experience profound shifts when they consciously gather in small groups and share from their hearts on topics that deeply affect them, and I believe the *Guide* can serve as a tool to help foster community and connection among mothers of all ages throughout the world.

As we've all discovered, there are many universal life themes that surface throughout the motherhood journey, so the playground for exploring these topics is expansive and fertile.

I hope you will carve out time in your life to invest in yourself and let the *Guide* support you in creating and living the life you truly desire—the life you deserve.

*The most precious gift you can give your child(ren) and partner is to love and nurture yourself first. Self-care is **not** about self-indulgence, it is about self-preservation.* It is not about pampering, it is about owning your personal power. It is about nurturing your potential and living the life you were meant to live.*

Warmly,
Renée

***Self-care is not about self-indulgence, it is about self-preservation.**

—Audre Lord

How to Get the Most from the *Guide*

Start or join a Personal Renewal Group (PRG). Motherhood can be an isolating experience. This is why the *Guide* is designed for women to use in a small group setting. While you can gain tremendous value from working on the themes and exercises on your own, being with a group and sharing your thoughts is what facilitates a change in how you **experience life and act on a daily basis.**

Be open. Some of the concepts and insights in the book may be new to you. If so, keep an open mind and be willing to look at things in a new way. If the concepts are familiar to you, be open to taking the themes to deeper levels.

Focus on what speaks to you and dive in. Depending on the age of your kids, your life stage and where you are on your personal growth journey, some themes will resonate with you more than others. Explore those topics/issues that bring tears to your eyes or make your heart swell.

Schedule the time to do the work. Each month when you explore new topics and work on the exercises, you're investing in yourself. The payoffs will be worth the investment (I promise!) if you'll take the time to follow through on the work.

Be honest. Your willingness to be truthful with yourself and others when exploring the *Guide*'s themes will support you in making progress on your path. Our willingness to be vulnerable is what allows us to access our own wisdom.

Let the theme permeate your month. The *Guide* is set up in a month-by-month format so you have a theme to work on and explore each month. Make the theme come alive for you! Talk about it with friends. Surround yourself with visual reminders—exercises, collages, pictures or quotes—by taping them up on your computer, your refrigerator or your bathroom mirror. Email other PRG moms about the topic or start a PRG listserv or an online group. Share the information with a close relative, your partner and friends.

Be easy on yourself. If you find yourself feeling overwhelmed by a particular chapter or exercise, that's okay. Give yourself permission to skip that section, come back to it later or go as slowly as you need to. You may not be ready to explore that theme quite yet. For many women, the months and years after having a child can be very overwhelming, and quite a few women experience anxiety and depression (see the end of the *Guide* for resources on managing depression). Be gentle with yourself and talk about your feelings with a friend, your PRG, or your ob-gyn, midwife or family doctor.

MANDALA ARTWORK

Throughout the *Guide* and on each chapter's title page, you'll see circular artwork. These intricate designs are called called "mandalas." Mandala is Sanskrit for sacred circle. Drawing and coloring mandalas is a widespread practice that often heightens personal insight, healing and self-expression. Coloring mandalas can be symbolic of undertaking a journey to the center of our being; often that which seemed dark or hidden and mysterious is illuminated. This exercise also helps many become more focused and feel more peaceful when they're struggling with personal issues.

Welcome

month one

Motherhood and Identity: Reconnecting with Who You Are

> Your ordinary self is enough.
> —Carol Orsborn, author

Having a baby changes you on a cellular level.

How you see, feel and think about everything in your life—relationships, career, spirituality, success, friendships, love—changes. You have joined a club that has a lifetime membership, and you'll never be the same "you" you were before baby.

I remember feeling awash with so many emotions and thoughts after having my son, Jonah.

I felt an intense need to protect and provide for this helpless baby, overwhelmed with the responsibility of our interdependence, worried (wondering, *am I doing this right?*) and dizzy from a rollercoaster of emotions I never knew I was capable of feeling!

Olympic Peninsula, Washington State

I remember a time when Jonah was about six weeks old. I left the house on a Saturday morning to go out and buy a new nursing bra while my husband stayed home with our newborn. As I sank into the car seat, feeling the strangeness of being truly alone for the first time in months, my mind raced to the absurd (but oddly alluring) thought, *I can actually just keep heading south and drive to Mexico!*

Then my engorged breasts reminded me of the errand before me.

As I pulled out of the driveway, I grabbed a CD (without looking to see who it was) and popped it into the CD player. The voice of Nanci Griffith, one of my favorite artists, filled the car. I turned up the radio almost as loud as it would go.

As I listened to the music I hadn't heard in over a year, I closed my eyes and let her voice and the melody wash over me. Tears rolled down my face as the music carried me to the "pre-baby" Renée. Being reminded of who I am—*who I was* before becoming a mom—brought up some sadness. I wondered if I would ever reconnect with this person who now felt like someone I used to know…and missed.

"Was the world still going on without me? Who had I become and where did I really belong?"

Depending on where we are on our life paths when we have kids, the journey of motherhood affects all of us differently, yet profoundly. Sometime between sleep deprivation, toilet training and homework, the question *who am I now?* will surface for just about every mother.

My good friend Amy describes feeling like an "interloper" the first time she and her baby daughter Haley left the house to go to the grocery store together. "After having the baby, I felt like I was frozen in time and space," she shares. "Was the world still going on without me? Who had I become and where did I really belong? It was a very strange feeling. My identity and sense of belonging, sense of place, felt completely in question."

While many agree that parenting is one of the most important jobs in life, none of us can be completely contained by one role.

It's often easy, though, to be so entirely consumed by our roles as mothers, we can forget that we're also *partners, daughters, sisters, granddaughters, friends, dancers, writers, athletes, teachers, lovers, mentors, volunteers, activists, leaders, artists, organizers, caregivers, managers and much, much more.*

Who you are cannot be contained or defined by a single role. We are, at our core, complex beings—and we become even more complex after having children.

How has your perception of **who you are** changed since becoming a parent?

Depending on where you are on your self-discovery journey, you may just need some regular time for quiet reflection and journaling to reconnect with your essence. Or you may feel a deeper need to reclaim your self and really figure out, for the first time, who you are and what you value—both as a woman and as a mother.

At a mom's night out I attended, we posed the question: "Is our goal then, post-baby, to return to the 'me' I used to be? Or is to let the experience of becoming a parent enrich and enhance who I am now and who I am becoming?" Regardless of our answers, we all agreed: *things would never be exactly the same.*

After my friend Amber, a successful freelance marketing consultant, had her first baby, she decided (after much discussion and planning) to stay home with her daughter during her first year and put work on hold.

She says she'll never forget the first time she was asked to introduce herself when visiting with a new group of mom friends and babies; she went blank and had to pause a minute. So much of her identity had been aligned with her role as an entrepreneur. Now she was "Anna's mom." A noble and wonderful role, but how strange it felt to slip on this new— and very different—skin.

As much as I connected with mom friends and loved children prior to becoming a mother, I don't think it's possible to fully understand the feelings associated with being a mom until you are one. I remember when my son was around four months old we went to a playgroup sponsored by the Association for Women in Communications, a professional organization with which I had been involved for almost fifteen years.

Sitting in a circle with these wonderful mentor moms—many of whom I had known for years through my work in the communications field—I felt a whole new sense of connection with them. Differences between us melted away, and my sense of *who I am* expanded as I began to integrate this new personae called mother.

For many moms, this transition period—integrating *who I was* with *who I am now*—can feel a little unsettling. (When it comes to any life transition, most of us, in general, are uncomfortable living in the unknown.)

> *"Reconnecting with myself by doing things I loved to do before I entered the pregnancy/baby world really helped me to relax into this new role."*

"I found it really helpful, when I was having my 'identity crisis' after Eli was born, to practice my violin one or two evenings a week, even for fifteen minutes," shares my friend Jennifer. "Reconnecting with myself by doing things I loved to do before I entered the pregnancy/baby world really helped me to relax into this new role."

What types of things did you love to do pre-baby that really made you feel alive, joyful and truly *you*?

Put on some of your favorite music, maybe something that reminds you of a memorable time in your life when you felt really happy and free. Go out to dinner with a girlfriend you've known for years but haven't seen in a while. Use these experiences to remember the activities that used to consume you prior to becoming pregnant. What are those things you enjoyed so immensely that they caused you to lose track of time? What types of causes did you volunteer for? What books, magazines or movies did you love to read or see?

A friend at my son's Montessori school has three children, ages five, three and six months. No doubt Lara, a professional opera singer and full-time mom, is juggling a lot, but she says what keeps her sane is her singing. "It reminds me of who I am," she says.

Nurturing your essence and sense of self is a wonderful way to teach your child(ren) the importance of individuality, expressing their life purpose and honoring their unique path.

GUIDED JOURNALING EXERCISE
Exploring Your Personal Values*

Set aside thirty minutes of quiet time to relax and get in touch with your " inner wisdom." Find a comfortable spot and move slowly through the following exercise. If you find it's hard to answer a question, that's okay. Just move on. These questions are not easy (in fact, they may be the most challenging ones you've ever answered), but the process will help you begin to reconnect with your true needs and desires. Give yourself some serious kudos when you finish this—it takes tremendous courage to really look within for these answers. **Note:** *You also may decide to complete this exercise at a leisurely pace during your solo date (see Self-Renewal Tip for the Month at the end of this chapter) or work on one exercise per week from this very important section.*

*Adapted in part from How to Find the Work You Love, *by Laurence G. Boldt. (www.empoweryou.com)*

What gifts do I want to share with others?

What is my heart's greatest desire?

What values are most important to me?

Who or what has had the greatest influence on my life?

Imagine yourself at the end of your life, filled with regret, with a painful sense of having not lived the life you wanted to live. What is it that you most regret not doing?

If you wrote a slogan for your philosophy of life, what would it be?

If you wrote an epitaph for your headstone, what might it say?

Is there anything unfinished in your life—personally or professionally—that you're willing to walk away from forever?

If you could take a six-month sabbatical alone (knowing that your child(ren) would be exquisitely cared for!), what would you do?

What do you envision your life to be like when you're sixty?

Find a picture of yourself between the ages of eight and thirteen that really captures your essence. Looking at this photo, write a letter to yourself (at the age you arc in the photo) using the self-guided letter on the next page.

Take this opportunity to connect with who you were then, acknowledging all the talents, gifts and attributes you can now see that maybe weren't so apparent to you at this young age.

When you finish, read it out loud and then post it somewhere you can see it throughout the month (bathroom, kitchen, office, etc.).

Renée, age 10

tape photo of yourself here

_____(Today's date)_____

Dear _____(your name)_____ , there are so many wonderful things I appreciate about you.

I am so proud of _____
_____

What I like best about you is _____
_____
_____

Nurture your interest in _____
_____
_____and don't forget to take time to _____
_____

Be loving and gentle with yourself, especially when it comes to _____
_____
_____

You have so many talents to share with others! Don't be afraid to _____
_____

Some of your innate qualities that will continually serve you on your life path are _____
_____

And remember, _____
_____

I honor who you are and commit to supporting you in fully expressing all your talents, potential and gifts.

Lovingly, your best friend

_____(your name)_____

SELF-RENEWAL TIP FOR THE MONTH
Take a Solo Date

WHAT: Go on a date with someone very special—you!

WHEN: Whenever you can manage to get a two- to three-hour (or longer) break. (The length of this break will, of course, depend on how old your child is and whether or not you're nursing.)

WHERE: See suggestions below (a contemplative setting is highly recommended).

BRING: Your journal, a pen and the exercises on the preceding pages, if you like.

TIPS: I strongly recommend that you don't go shopping, run errands or go to a movie. This date is your time just to be totally alone, be still and create some space to reflect and let whatever comes up, come up.

Here are some suggestions for solo dates:

- Go to a nearby spring or favorite swimming spot (depending on the weather!).

- Go hang out at a coffeehouse: these should be listed on your local newspaper's Web site in the food/entertainment section. You'll also find lots of coffeehouses near universities or colleges.

- Go to a deli or natural foods store and pick up items for a delicious picnic. Bring your treats to a local park and enjoy them under a shady tree.

- Go to your favorite bookstore and browse the career, self-improvement, women's health, psychology and spirituality sections. Take note of what topics are most interesting or appealing to you. Make sure you take time to be quiet, and, if you like, sip on a relaxing beverage. Resist the urge to turn this into a shopping trip; this is your time to reflect.

- Go to an ice cream or yogurt store and get a special treat. Enjoy a sundae while you sit outside and journal.

- Go for a relaxing walk in nature, perhaps near a local lake, river or pond.

- Write a poem about your life and how it's changed since having your baby.

- Visit the Inspiration Café at www.careerstrategists.net (Renée's company Web site) and try some of the exercises listed under Passion Play.

- Try a yoga or NIA class (www.nia-nia.com) and then treat yourself to a strawberry-peach smoothie afterward.

- Go to a bookstore or gift store and buy yourself a new journal. Take time to break it in while reflecting on the guided journaling exercise and sipping on green tea.

- Go to one of your favorite outdoor spots to relax and journal on twenty things you're grateful for.

- Go to a wine bar and have a glass of your favorite wine while making a list of your favorite things about yourself.

- If it's rainy, use your imagination: where can you find a cozy, quiet kid-free corner to relax, journal and reflect? Hmmm.

Really enjoy this opportunity to be alone with your wonderful self. Many moms share that they have major revelations about their life and feel much clearer and focused after these solo dates.

RECOMMENDED RESOURCES

The Sacrificial Mother: Escaping the Trap of Self-Denial,
by Carin Rubenstein, PhD

Surrendering to Motherhood: Losing Your Mind, Finding Your Soul,
by Iris Krasnow

Motherless Mothers and *Motherless Daughters*, by Hope Edelman

The Mother Dance: How Children Change Your Life, by Harriet Lerner

Resources for mothers managing depression
(see "Resources to Support You" at the end of the *Guide*)

Tips on journaling
(see "Resources to Support You" at the end of the *Guide*)

REFLECTIONS ON
Reconnecting with Who You Are

Use this space to expand on your thoughts and feelings around this topic. See
"Tips on Journaling" at the end of the *Guide* for support if you're new to journaling.

THE POWER OF SELF-CARE

The demands of mothering (and nursing), particularly when your kids are young, are great. Often, despite their good intentions, your partner or family members just don't understand how much physical/emotional energy it takes to care for and nurse a newborn, or to take care of children, period. When you begin to think about self-care and getting in touch with your own needs, you realize there are times when you're the only one who really knows <u>what</u> you need to be/feel your best. And you have to stand up for your own needs, despite outside influences. The bottom line is that there are many times a nursing mom needs to sleep—and let the dishes go. More and more I'm starting to be able to recognize this and be okay with it. Self-care was not something most of us were taught—it's something we have to learn. Baby steps.

—Lara, mom to Maddie, six, Rowan, three, and Hoyt, one

month two

The Transformative Power of Self-Care

You can explore the universe looking for somebody who is more deserving of your love and affection than you are yourself, and you will not find that person anywhere.

—Anonymous

Growing up as the oldest of seven children (five boys and two girls), I remember breakfast at our house being extremely hectic.

My harried mom was scrambling to make lunches, my dad was running around looking for tennis shoes and invariably one of the seven of us was in the kitchen cooking peanut butter oatmeal, rice flour pineapple muffins or some other strange concoction (in our family we were heartily encouraged to become masterful at "life skills"—this philosophy encouraged lots of cooking experiments but invariably led to mayhem in the kitchen!).

One morning my nine-year-old brother, Kert (now a macrobiotic chef), decided to whip up some pecan waffles. As I reached over to the waffle

Vancouver, BC, Canada

maker to help myself to breakfast, I bumped the edge of the hot grill and burned my elbow. I must have been ten years old at the time.

I don't remember if I mentioned the accident to my parents, but hours later I was sitting in my classroom at school, trying to ignore the pain from a small, brown, bubbly-looking burn on my elbow.

Rather than go and get a teacher for help or a bandage, I simply suffered, thinking silently, *it's not really important enough to bother anyone.*

Self-care is about nurturing yourself on all levels—physically, mentally, emotionally and spiritually—so you can live, love and parent optimally.

This is my earliest recollection of realizing that self-care was not something that was promoted or taught in my family (even though my parents were medical professionals!). It was definitely something I had to learn.

Maybe when you think of self-care, you have visions of pedicures and facials. Indeed, physical self-care is a big part of the overall picture. But eliminating critical thinking, not over-scheduling, releasing the need to be perfect, hiring a babysitter for dates with your partner or yourself, saying no, refusing to do things out of guilt and giving yourself much-needed rest and downtime to refuel are also integral to total self-care.

Self-care is about nurturing yourself on all levels—physically, mentally, emotionally and spiritually—so you can live, love and parent optimally.

Visiting with my friend Megan, mom to Mateo, three, and Alea, one, I listened as she shared how frustrated she was feeling. Exhausted from staying up until two a.m. the night before to do laundry, she had skipped breakfast and lunch, was surviving on nothing but coffee and had been beating herself up all day about not getting a homemade meal over to her neighbor, who had recently lost her father. My heart ached for Megan. Most of us would never imagine denying our children of sleep or nourishment, being judgmental of them or allowing them to ignore their emotional needs.

Yet, as mothers, we do this to ourselves on a daily basis.

The same love, gentle care and compassion we offer so generously to our little ones should be extended to ourselves as well. We teach our children about self-worth and honoring one's value through our actions, not our words. Modeling self-love and self-acceptance is the most effective way to have a powerful impact on a child's self-esteem and how they view themselves.

Below are several examples of how you can begin nurturing yourself and start making self-renewal part of your everyday life.

Physical Care

- Be kind and loving to your body—appreciate your body.

- Nourish your body by eating healthy and energizing foods that make you feel great.

- Get enough sleep and drink plenty of water to stay hydrated.

- Exercise to replenish your energy and manage stress.

- Take time to enjoy, nurture and appreciate your physical appearance.

Emotional Care

- Have a heart-to-heart with a close friend or mentor.

- Have kind, loving thoughts about yourself (try no criticism for one week!).

- Seek out support from a therapist, coach, social worker or counselor.

- Journal—write down your feelings and thoughts.

- Go on a fun date alone or with your partner or organize a monthly girls' night out.

Spiritual Care

- Take time to be by yourself to think or write.

- Take a walk in a park or out in nature.

- Meditate, pray or just reflect on what you're grateful for.

- Do something creative: paint/draw/write/dance/sing.

- Volunteer for a cause you're passionate about.

Mental Care

- Read a good book or see an intellectually stimulating movie.

- Learn a new hobby or skill.

- Sign up for a class, group or workshop on a topic that is interesting to you.

- Challenge yourself within your community or at work to learn something new.

Almost any mother will share with you how pervasive ideals like *good mothers always put their families first, motherhood is pure bliss, you just have to let your body go when you become a mom* or *good mothers are completely selfless* abound in our society.

These beliefs run deep—even if they're not on a conscious level and you don't buy into them—and can have a profound impact on how we view our roles as mothers and women. Realize this and be aware that the concept of self-care may feel foreign and difficult to embrace at first (to say the least).

Why Self-Care?

What are some reasons that self-care is important and how do we benefit by making time for self-renewal?

- By filling our cups first, we tend to feel more generous and can avoid building resentments toward others who demand our energy and time.

- Nurturing ourselves makes us naturally feel more loving, which makes us better friends, partners, parents and more fun to be around!

- Making our self-care a priority is one of the best ways to validate and honor our own worth, which naturally enhances true confidence and self-esteem.

- Taking care of ourselves on all levels (physically/mentally/emotionally/ spiritually) helps us feel alive and whole, able to function at our best and do all the things we want to do.

- By taking time to care for ourselves, we renew and restore our energy supply and create energy reserves so we're able to weather unforeseen challenges more easily.

- Practicing self-care and being loving and gentle toward ourselves helps us to be more present and calm, so we can respond wisely, intuitively and effectively to a variety of circumstances.

- Honoring and nurturing our essence provides us with opportunities to experience profound spiritual and personal growth.

- Owning our personal power (realizing our potential) is our birthright. Self-care, self-love and self-acceptance are wonderful avenues for reaching this goal.

- When you feel good on the inside, you look good on the outside. Nurturing your essence—inside and out—promotes overall well-being and a sense of vitality.

For me, having grown up with a mother who suffered from depression and struggled constantly with issues around self-worth and self-esteem, I am motivated to make self-care an important part of my life so I can model this behavior for my son. I want him to see the value of total self-care and how it can positively impact how he feels about himself and others.

Self-care is not about pampering. It's about owning your personal power. It's about self-worth and honoring the person you are.

After you taste the benefits of focusing on your self-care, you will begin to schedule time for self-nurturing just like you schedule doctor or dentist appointments. You'll discover that it is integral to your emotional survival and that you are wiser and more effective in all areas of your life when you take time to fill your cup first!

"The other night at dinner my husband commented on how much more relaxed and joyful I seemed since I had started exercising and taking 'journaling dates,'" shares Ella. "And since I started taking time for me, I also felt more generous and playful with my kids."

The changes she made in her life inspired her husband to focus on his self-care, and now he takes guitar classes every Wednesday night. Ella uses the free evening to connect with other moms/kids whose partners also claim Wednesday night for their solo dates. The women have dubbed these regular dinners out as the "Wednesday Night Widows Club," and all involved look forward to and relish these weekly community gatherings.

The journey to making your self-care a priority (and understanding how life-altering it can be) doesn't happen overnight.

The journey to making your self-care a priority (and understanding how life-altering it can be) doesn't happen overnight. Remember, many women who initially equate self-care with selfishness may require a shift in thinking to make this an everyday practice. Be gentle, compassionate and understanding with yourself and know that you are doing the best you can wherever you are on your journey.

Now friend, what do *you* need to live, love and parent optimally?

GUIDED JOURNALING EXERCISE
Making Your Self-Care a Priority

Set aside twenty minutes for some quiet reflection. Get comfortable, put on your coziest clothes or make some hot or iced herbal tea for yourself. Have your journal nearby in case you want to elaborate on the exercise below. If the concept of self-care is new to you, take it slowly and ease into this.

What do **you** need (physically, emotionally, spiritually and mentally) to be the best person, mom and partner you can be? Remember, each person's response will be vastly different.

What steps can you begin to take this month to make your self-care a priority?

(1)

(2)

(3)

What changes are you willing to implement today to start making self-care integral to your week?

What would motivate you to make your self-renewal a priority?

Look at the *Why Self-Care* list and list your top three reasons for practicing self-care.

(1)

(2)

(3)

TAKE ACTION
Jump-Start Your Self-Care Routine

Call and set up a dinner or coffee date with a friend, either from your PRG or another trusted advocate. If the friend is not in your PRG and you think they'd enjoy it, share the chapter exercise with them before your date. When you meet, take turns reading your answers to the questions above. Be specific when answering the question, "What steps can you begin to take this month to make your self-care a priority?"

Over the course of the month, notice when and if you think about self-care. If it does cross your radar, notice when this occurs.

Check in with your friend thirty days after your date to see how your self-care practice is going (or once a week via email or phone if you can). Be easy on yourself. And remember, baby steps.

SELF-RENEWAL TIP FOR THE MONTH
Your Morning Check-Up

For the next thirty days, every morning before you step out of bed, take two minutes to gently scan your body and check how you're feeling. Ask yourself, *What do I need to feel nurtured and to function at my best TODAY?*

Remember the four areas of self-care: emotional, physical, mental and spiritual. Make it a priority to address whatever comes up for you, even if it means saying "no" to something or altering your schedule for the day. Maybe you need a massage or to go for a walk. Perhaps you need to eliminate caffeine or sugar, get more sleep, start taking weekly solo dates or find a therapist or a coach for support on relationship or career issues. Maybe you need to go to dinner with a girlfriend you haven't seen in a while and reconnect. Just taking a minute to do a self-care checkup sends a message to yourself that you're committed to your well-being. Your life will begin to radically change once you start to feel loved, nurtured and truly in tune with your own needs. And your child(ren) and family will benefit immeasurably!

RECOMMENDED RESOURCES

The Women's Comfort Book, by Jennifer Louden (www.comfortqueen.com)

Energy Addict: 101 Physical, Mental, and Spiritual Ways to Energize Your Life, by Jon Gordon (www.jongordon.com)

Life Makeovers: 52 Practical & Inspiring Ways to Improve Your Life One Week at a Time, by Cheryl Richardson (www.cherylrichardson.com)

Women's Bodies, Women's Wisdom and *Mother-Daughter Wisdom*, by Christiane Northrup (www.drnorthrup.com)

Eight Weeks to Optimum Health, by Dr. Andrew Weil (www.drweil.com)

REFLECTIONS ON SELF-CARE

Use this space to expand on your thoughts and feelings around this topic. See "Tips on Journaling" at the end of the *Guide* for support if you're new to journaling.

_____

_____

_____

_____

_____

_____

_____

THE POWER OF SELF-CARE

After the birth of two children, I was carrying around some extra weight. To say I was not an athletic person would be putting it mildly. I used to joke that the only time I would run would be so I could stand first in line for the buffet. My physical well-being had definitely taken a backseat to the care and nurturing of my kids. After focusing for quite a while on the self-care message, I decided to take a big step, and when a woman in my Personal Renewal Group said she needed a walking partner, I raised my hand. That next week we set off with my kids in tow. As we walked each week, the weight began to drop off, and my friendship with my walking partner grew. The confidence I found inspired me to train for and participate in my first Danskin Triathlon. My walking partner was there with me all the way, as were the other PRG moms, providing encouragement and support. I felt such pride following the race. It took a lot of training and a few sacrifices along the way, but the experience taught me so much about my internal power and myself. I now understand that acknowledging and addressing my needs (physical, emotional and spiritual) is not a weakness, it is a priority.

—Kelli, mom to Jackson, six, and Lauren, three

month three

Creating Your Personal Support System

Enlisting the help of a robust support network makes all the difference in how you experience your journey.

—Anonymous

When Jonah was two, we attended his friend Gabriel's birthday party. Moms and toddlers were sitting outside in the family's large, tree-covered backyard eating pizza on blankets, talking about the lack of support many of us were feeling in our lives.

My friend Ana, who grew up in Peru, had recently returned from an extended stay in her native country with her one-year-old. Ana told us she loved going home because in her culture, caring for children was a responsibility shared not only by her extended family, but by their village as well. In fact, she said, when it was necessary, it was not uncommon for women even to nurse one another's babies.

In many countries around the world, talking about creating a personal support system would be a bizarre and foreign conversation topic. But in

Florence, Italy

our western culture, where we work so hard to stress independence from a very early age (the first question you are asked after you have a baby is "is he sleeping through the night yet?"), we're often made to feel as if reaching out and asking for help is a sign of weakness.

Recently, while at a major fast food chain getting a drink from the water fountain, I noticed a promotional poster on the wall advertising their products. The poster was comparing their "strong burrito" to attributes of a "strong person." At the top of the list of desirable traits was "doesn't need to ask for help."

With messages like this bombarding us everywhere we go, it's no wonder we're so determined to go it alone.

When you've been up all night with a sick child, are feeling insecure about your parenting ability, are feeling disconnected from your partner, are having a hard time adjusting to a new boss or role at work, or are feeling overwhelmed and frustrated with all the balls you're juggling, who do you call?

Do you have friends who are always there for you, who will support you when you're down? Other parents who can act as mentors and help you through difficult times? Professional colleagues or peers who can coach you on how to handle a tough career or interpersonal communication challenge? Or groups that meet to share ideas and connect through meaningful dialogue?

When I first became a mom, I remember how hard it was for me—a type A overachiever with controlling tendencies—to make the switch from being ultra independent to asking for help from my husband, peers, friends, mentors and family.

I distinctly remember the day when my husband, John, returned to work after having been home with me for two weeks with our newborn.

Sitting in my quiet kitchen, listening to the clock tick and blanketed in a postpartum haze, I realized, *this is it, I'm all alone. With a baby!* It was a very lonely and scary realization, and I have never felt the absence of a support system more than I did then.

During the summer of 2005, I lost my maternal grandmother, a strong, entrepreneurial spirit who died at age ninety-three. My paternal grandmother, an eccentric, flamboyant rancher, followed her shortly thereafter at age eighty-seven. As the months and years pass, I continue to unwrap (and be surprised by) the many gifts my mother and grandmothers passed on to me. Yet, with all their strengths and abilities, the one thing that I had to teach myself was that I didn't have to go it alone. I could ask for help.

The one thing that I had to teach myself was that I didn't have to go it alone. I could ask for help.

My journey to learning to ask for support was a slow one. But one motivation to make this change came through observing others. I started to notice that people I really admired—those who seemed to experience more balance, integration and true emotional health and resiliency—had strong support systems in place and were comfortable stating their needs and asking others for help. I didn't think they were weak at all—I really admired them!

"When Bryan goes out of town for work for the week or longer, I know things will be more challenging as I'll be solo parenting," shares Sarah, mom to two toddlers. "I have learned these are the times I need to heap on the extra support. I usually ask my younger sister to babysit one night during the week so I can enjoy a quiet dinner out with a girlfriend, and I have our high school neighbor come over from four to seven p.m. three nights during the week to help with dinner, baths and bedtime. I also make sure I have lots of frozen dinners or easy-to-prepare food in the house. I used to dread these business trips and would want to dump the kids on my husband the minute he returned from his trip. Now I have learned that I just have to build in extra support when he's away on a trip." She adds, "Not only is the week more peaceful and enjoyable, but my husband returns to a family that's happy to see him, rather than being resentful that he's been gone."

What Are the Benefits of Having a Support Network?

Having a support system can have a huge impact on how you experience day-to-day life. Research shows that individuals with robust support systems:

- are more effective at work and at home (they feel as if they have a team behind them and that they're not all alone)

- keep resolutions, particularly those involving their health and physical well-being

- weather personal and professional challenges more easily

- are less likely to feel overwhelmed and find it easier to maintain perspective

- stay healthier on all levels—mentally, physically and emotionally

- are less likely to feel isolated (isolation can lead to feelings of despair and failure)

- experience less stress and burnout

- have children who are comfortable asking for and receiving support and help from others

It took a long time, but I finally started to see that feeling supported while moving through a transition or facing a challenging issue can make all the difference in how you experience the journey—and how your family experiences the journey as well.

What do you need to do to create a strong, nurturing support system that will be available for you, regardless of the challenge—whether it is related to parenting, your career or a relationship issue? Maybe you just need to cultivate an existing friendship. Reach out to someone who has offered the help before. Ask a potential mentor to lunch. Or take action and create a support group that will meet your specific needs.

We all need support—lots of it. We weren't meant to do everything for ourselves. Assess how you navigate challenges: do you immediately jump into a one-person rowboat and head out to sea to battle the choppy waters alone? Or do you thoughtfully enlist the help of fellow passengers who have already weathered similar challenges? The choice is in your hands.

GUIDED JOURNALING EXERCISE
Asking for Help

Schedule a twenty-minute break to further explore this topic. Have your journal nearby to record any additional ideas or thoughts that come up around this topic. Share your answers with a friend or your partner.

How do I feel when I think about reaching out and asking others for help?

What limiting beliefs or thoughts do I need to release in order to become comfortable asking for help?

Who in my life is good at utilizing a support system, and what do I admire about them?

How would I feel if I were completely supported and nurtured by a robust support network? How would my life look different?

Take out a large oversized sheet of paper, draw an oversized circle and put a recent photograph of yourself in the middle of the circle. Using colored pens or pencils, create lines or "rays of support" radiating out from you to the outer edges of the circle (like spokes on a wagon wheel). Then, referencing the list on the following page, fill in the lines and create your ideal personal support system. It may be helpful to divide your support wheel into four categories such as work (or community), self, family/marriage and household.

Everyone's support system will look different; this is about what *you* need to feel fully supported where you are right now!

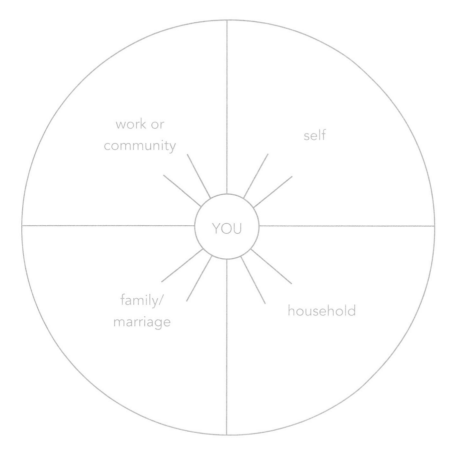

Following is a list of individuals you may consider to be part of your support network (now or in the future).

Your support system may include:

- Professional/personal mentors

- Professional development and networking organizations

- Professional or skills-based teachers, instructors or trainers

- Work/life balance, business or career coach

- Professional peers/colleagues

- Friends with kids

- Friends without kids

- Neighbors

- Playgroups

- Parenting groups/support and parenting coach

- Single parent organizations

- Babysitting and child care co-ops (start one in your neighborhood or city)

- Child care providers (day care, Mother's Day Out programs, sitting or nanny services, child care co-ops, list of babysitters, etc.) and pediatricians

- Social groups; creative or book/hobby groups; activities just for women or moms

- Therapist, counselor and/or support groups

- Spiritual mentors/groups or community

- Financial consultants or advisors

- Online support communities, teleclasses, etc.

- Family members

- Meal co-ops (start one in your neighborhood) and meal delivery programs

- Personal errand service (some of these start at very reasonable hourly rates)

- Home care/cleaning and yard care help

- Bodywork and women's health specialists (physicians, ob-gyns, midwives, chiropractors, acupuncturists, menopause/hormone health specialists, nutritionists, personal trainers, massage therapists, etc.)

A few things to keep in mind when creating your support network:

- Remember, everyone's support system will look different; this is about what you need to feel fully supported at your current life stage.

- Your support system will change depending on your life stage, current needs and the age of your children and parents (if you're involved in their care as well).

- Choose friends or colleagues you admire for their experience and insight to be a part of your support system. Enlist the support of those whose lives reflect the values and beliefs you admire.

- Your support system may or may not include your family—they are only one of the many resources listed above! (In fact, many people may find it difficult or unhealthy to enlist their family as part of their support network.)

- Consider how you want to turn this support wheel into something you'll use every day (a list of phone numbers you keep in your purse, by your computer, on a bulletin board at home, etc.). It is often reassuring to have these names/numbers at arm's reach.

Share your support system drawing with your partner or a friend (and encourage them to create their own support wheel). Post this drawing where you can see it and where it can remind you that help and support are only a phone call away.

I have a special support bulletin board in my kitchen with a picture of my family in the middle and an affirmation in large type at the top of the board that reads "I Manage My Life with Ease and I Experience an Abundance of Time and Support." On the board, I have posted lists of various support areas with phone numbers (moms/friends, playgroups, health and body care, babysitters/child care, housecleaner, etc.). It really helps me to have this information handy, but more importantly, I feel supported just by looking at the board and being able to visualize my support system, ready to spring into action when needed.

SELF-RENEWAL TIP FOR THE MONTH
Home Alone

Ask your partner or a friend to take your child(ren) for a couple of hours on a Saturday or Sunday morning or afternoon so you can spend time AT HOME alone. Many mothers share how rare it is to be at home alone, yet they can't believe how much they missed and enjoy this opportunity. Take time to make yourself a cup of tea and write in your journal, sit on your back patio, make yourself a gourmet breakfast, take a nap in your own bed (silence, ahhhh), soak in the bathtub or just put on some of your favorite music and turn it up as loud as you want and dance. Really enjoy the time and just relax. Resist the urge to clean or do household chores. Notice how this little break nourishes and refuels you and how excited you are to see your children when they return. Offer to allow your partner to experience the same break. I know some couples who take turns once a month going on overnight trips with the kids so their partner can be home alone for twenty-four hours. They say that it not only keeps them sane, it's rejuvenating and good for the whole family.

RECOMMENDED RESOURCES

Start or join a Personal Renewal Group: visit www.reneetrudeau.com or see "How to Start Your Own Personal Renewal Group" at the end of the *Guide*.

Find or start a playgroup: see Mothers of Preschoolers (www.mops.org), or view additional resources at www.mothersandmore.org (for mothers transitioning into or out of the workplace) or www.momsclub.com (for stay-at-home mothers).

Find a career, life or business coach: www.coachfederation.org or www.coachville.com.

Find a therapist: ask for a referral from your physician or friends. Also, try The American Psychological Association's Web site: www.apa.org and look for the *Find a Psychologist* link on the home page. Visit www.agpa.org, the American Group Psychotherapy Association's Web site for a listing of group therapists (a great resource for women who need help and want to connect with other women). And learn more about and find an Imago therapist in your community at www.imagorelationships.org.

Find help with meal planning: www.savingdinner.com.

Use this space to expand on your thoughts and feelings around this topic. See "Tips on Journaling" at the end of the *Guide* for support if you're new to journaling.

_____

_____

_____

_____

_____

_____

_____

THE POWER OF SELF-CARE

Once a week, my husband and I sit down and plan our week and look at where we need help. The idea of utilizing a support system used to be foreign to me—I did everything on my own. Now, we are always on the same page and it feels so great to be connected to him. (And our kids love to see a happy mommy and daddy.) Before we did this, we were frustrated and disjointed. Asking for help and seeking support can be hard at first—but it's well worth the effort!

—Rebecca, mom to Alex, five, and Piper, three

Building a support system has been one of the best things I've done for myself in a long time. Being a first-time mom and living in a new city was tough on me and my spouse. Having a support group gave me a renewed confidence in myself and helped me to focus on what was really important: me, my spouse and our new baby boy. I struggled a lot (and still do) with asking for help, but I have realized I can't do it alone. Just recently I lost my caregiver for my child. Before I became comfortable using my support network, I would have panicked and felt totally out of control. Instead, by talking to other moms in similar situations, I learned to focus on what was important, practiced 'good is good enough' and asked for help like you wouldn't believe; I even flew in a friend from Oklahoma to watch my son for a week while I was at work! Every day I'm becoming more comfortable reaching out and asking for help.

—Angela, mom to Cole, nine months

month four

Managing Your Energy: Setting Priorities, Saying No and Asking for Help

Things which matter most must never be at the mercy of things which matter least.

—Johann Wolfgang von Goethe, poet/philosopher

Who or what receives the majority of your attention, time and energy?

Your husband? Your kids? Your work? Your household? Worries? Finances? Friendships? Volunteer activities? Hobbies?

One spring when I was in my late twenties—a time when I frequently took evening art classes—I enrolled in a black and white photography class at a local arts center in downtown Austin.

Once a week I rushed from my corporate public relations job, where I handled international media relations, and fought congested traffic to make it to my class at the other end of town. Hurrying in one evening, I apologized to my good-looking, forty-something instructor for being late and told him that although I had hoped to get to the darkroom earlier to

---

Yosemite National Park – Sierra Nevada, California

work on my printmaking, it just wasn't possible with my work demands. He shrugged, "Well, it was a choice you made."

"No," I protested (a little too vehemently), "you don't understand! I had to lead a satellite media tour for German press today and had five back-to-back meetings and ten phone calls to return before I could leave." (And this was before email was huge, if you can imagine!)

Again, he stated, smiling, "It was your choice."

I started to protest again, thinking, *this guy is really out of touch with reality.* Then I became silent as the truth of his words—as irksome as they were—slowly seeped in. As hard as it was for me to accept, I did have a choice. We all do. And I had chosen where I lived, where and how I worked, and what my priorities were. I wasn't a puppet on strings; I had set up my life and made the choices that brought me to where I was at the time.

We each have a finite amount of energy, time and resources. Most of us "give away" and waste our energy every day without even realizing it—through lengthy, unfulfilling or sometimes unnecessary phone conversations; endless time on email, the Web or watching TV; tolerating disorganized spaces that cause us to spend hours looking for items; going to social gatherings or volunteer events that we don't want to attend but feel we should attend, and on and on.

> I wasn't a puppet on strings; I had set up my life and made the choices that brought me to where I was at the time.

What we often don't realize is that these activities deplete our valuable energy bank.

Not only are these activities unfulfilling—and often draining—but they are zapping our precious energy and resources and keeping us from spending time on things that truly fuel us—like being with friends, enjoying our children, spending time outdoors or connecting with our partners.

It would be ideal for all of us to have an overflow or abundance of energy—what I like to call energy reserves. So, whenever we hit a crisis or bump in the road, we could navigate these challenges more easily without becoming totally energy-depleted, which can lead to stress, sickness, depression, anxiety or worse.

Think about key areas of your life: your relationship with your partner or other family members, your role as a parent, your financial state, your spiritual health, your friendships, your household, your emotional or physical well-being, your career or community work.

What are your *top life priorities* (meaning what is on your radar right now), and does the way you allocate your time and energy reflect these choices?

GUIDED JOURNALING EXERCISE
Top Life Priorities

Schedule a twenty-minute break to further explore this topic. Have your journal nearby to record any additional ideas or thoughts that come up around this topic. Share your answers with a friend or your partner.

My top (three) life priorities based on how <u>I currently allocate my energy and resources</u> are:

(1)

(2)

(3)

Reflect on this list and then create a new list based on how you would like to direct your energy over the next three months. (It's a good idea to update this list every ninety days as life stages and family circumstances continually change.) What in your life is calling for your attention *right now*?

My new top (three) life priorities for the next ninety days are:

(1)

(2)

(3)

The next time you are considering a new work, family or volunteer/community project or commitment, remember that while it may be important, it will take time and valuable energy away from your other priorities. Pause, look at the list above and ask yourself: *Can I afford to do this, or will the added stress be too taxing on my personal or my family's well-being?*

You always have a choice, and when you're an active parent with a busy life and children who need a lot of your energy, you must be cautious before committing to activities that are not on your Top Life Priorities list.

Say Yes to Saying No

Based on the way we as women are socialized—to put others first, to be the nurturers, to be selfless—one of the hardest things for many of us to do is to say *no*.

Often it's helpful to look at why we have such a hard time with this. The explanation is different for each of us and has a lot to do with how we were raised and who we are as individuals. Consider the list below and see if any of these points resonate with you.

Common reasons many women have trouble saying no or asking for help:

- Fear of disappointing others (do you suffer from the disease to please?)

- Fear of failure

- Fear of the reaction of others

- An inability to receive support (you may ask, *do I deserve this?*)

- Fear of rejection

- Fear of being judged or criticized (for some, asking for help may be viewed as a weakness)

Creative Ways to Say No

To encourage you in your newfound skill, here is a great list of nine creative ways to say no. I promise, the more you say no, the lighter and more free you'll feel and the easier it will become to draw clear boundaries that support you.

(1) **Just No:** "Thanks, I'll have to pass on that." (Say it, then shut up.)

(2) **The Gracious No:** "I really appreciate you asking me, but my time is already committed."

(3) **The "I'm Sorry" No:** "I wish I could, but it's just not going to work right now."

(4) **The "It's Someone Else's Decision" No:** "I promised my coach (therapist, etc.) I wouldn't take on any more projects right now. I'm working on creating more balance in my life."

(5) **The "My Family is the Reason" No:** "Thanks so much for the invite, that's the day of my son's soccer game, and I never miss those."

(6) **The "I Know Someone Else" No:** "I just don't have time right now. Let me recommend someone who may be able to help you."

(7) **The "I'm Already Booked" No:** "I appreciate you thinking of me, but I'm afraid I'm already booked that day."

(8) **The "Setting Boundaries" No:** "Let me tell you what I *can* do ..." Then limit the commitment to what will be comfortable for you.

(9) **The "Not No, But Not Yes" No:** "Let me think about it, and I'll get back to you."

(This list is adapted in part from *Work Less, Make More—Stop Working So Hard and Create the Life You Really Want*, by Jennifer White.)

Tips to Help You Manage Your Energy More Effectively

- Become proficient and comfortable at saying no. Practice it. Challenge yourself to say no at least once a week to a request that is not directly aligned with your Top Life Priorities. Many mothers agree that having a child is often incredibly freeing in that they become clearer on their priorities and find it easier to say no to non-essential activities that pull them away from their family.

- Ask for help—frequently! Successful, balanced people have robust support systems. And support is only a phone call away. Asking for support takes practice if you are used to being highly independent. Successful parenting requires interdependence (and isn't this something you want to model for your child?). Start small—do a child care swap with a neighbor. I promise, the more you ask for and receive help, the easier it gets. And you'll be an inspiration to your friends to practice asking for and receiving help as well!

- Challenge "shoulds" when they surface in your mind. They are always a red flag that you're about to do something not because you want to, but because you feel pressure from an outside influence to do so. Pause and reflect before you take action and ask, *what is my motivation for taking on this new activity?*

- Give yourself permission to change your mind at any time! Period. Too many of us are continually committing to things we think we *should* do instead of things we *want* to do. You always have the right to let someone know you have reconsidered a request and really can't take on another commitment at this time.

Do you want more clarity and focus in your life? A short time away alone might be just the thing you need to sweep away the mental cobwebs and get crystal clear on your life direction.

Consider setting aside an entire day—completely void of all distractions—for a personal life planning retreat. Use this time to get clear on your priorities and to think about how you want to allocate your energy and resources over the next ninety days *(this is a great time to work on the previous exercises).*

Spend some time thinking about and listing what activities fuel you (which ones give you energy, nurture you, fill you with passion) and what activities drain you (those things that create a physical tightness or discomfort in your back, belly or neck every time they cross your consciousness). Often these drains are things like a financial issue that must be handled, a tough conversation that has been postponed, a disorganized space at work or at home or a project that has been on the back burner for too long. I like to approach these items with an aggressive housecleaning mindset, giving myself three options to eliminate these drains:

(1)   I can **do it**—set deadlines for completion of the project

(2)   I can **delegate it**—ask for help if needed or outsource the task

(3)   I can **dump it**—make the decision that I'm ready to walk away from this task and release that it just isn't going to happen (at least not this year!)

During your personal planning retreat, you can revisit old goals or dreams, enlist books for inspiration (see the "Recommended Resources" at the end of each chapter or the reading list at the end of the *Guide* for recommendations), work on exercises, journal, draw/paint or create a collage that represents your vision for how you want to experience the next three months. Do whatever motivates you and helps you gain clarity.

A primary goal of this mini-retreat is to give your analytical thinking a rest and give your creativity and your inner compass the opportunity to have a voice.

Some tips to help you get the most from your retreat

- Spend at least four hours away (a twenty-four-hour retreat would be ideal).

- Choose a location that is inspiring and conducive to contemplation—a quiet park or natural setting; a friend's vacant house; a retreat, yoga or spa center or even a quiet coffeehouse are good places to go (but get out of your own house!).

- Focus on what you want to create for the next ninety days of your life.

I recommend taking personal planning retreats two to four times a year, if at all possible. These retreats are a wonderful, nurturing way for you to invest in yourself and your future. They may just be one of the best gifts you'll ever receive! Have fun, and make this your own.

Purchase some lavender essential oil* at a local natural foods store or from an aromatherapist or massage therapist (lavender oil actually has many uses in addition to the calming effect that is inherent to this flower). In the evening, after the house is quiet, draw a hot bath and add some lavender oil. If you like, pour yourself a cool glass of water or make a cup of hot peppermint tea to enjoy while you bathe. Breathe. Relax. Take your time lingering in the warmth and appreciating your strong, wonderful, miraculous body and all that it does for you and the many ways that it nurtures your family. Think of all the things you appreciate about your body and its many abilities—your strong back, your agile feet, your amazing hands and fingers, your beautiful breasts, your soft skin, your sweet belly and your miraculous eyes and ears. After your bath, choose a favorite lotion and take a few minutes to gently give yourself a foot and hand massage, acknowledging your hands and feet for all the work they do. Try taking a "body appreciation bath" once a week. It's a great way to end a busy day.

*You can also visit www.auracacia.com to purchase essential oils.

RECOMMENDED RESOURCES

The Joy Diet, by Martha Beck (www.marthabeck.com)

Slowing Down to the Speed of Life: How to Create a More Peaceful, Simpler Life from the Inside Out, by Richard Carlson and Joseph Bailey

The Speed Trap: How to Avoid the Frenzy of the Fast Lane, by Joseph Bailey

Work Less, Make More: Stop Working So Hard and Create the Life You Really Want, by Jennifer White

The Power of Intention, by Wayne W. Dyer

Use this space to expand on your thoughts and feelings around this topic. See "Tips on Journaling" at the end of the *Guide* for support if you're new to journaling.

THE POWER OF SELF-CARE

One night, after discussing reasons why and ways to say "no" during an evening session with my PRG, I paired off with another self-employed mom. We compared current work projects, including those that were eating our time (already at a premium as we both work from home with limited child care) without financial or personal reward. I told my PRG buddy about an upcoming project for a high-profile company—a financially lucrative assignment about which I was not terribly excited. I shook my head as I told her, "but I can't say no to it."

On the drive home I thought more about our conversation and what was really important to me. I decided that I could say no to this project and thus free up more time for my sons, both of whom really needed me that month. I called the clients the next day and told them that I had several prior commitments and could not do their project but would be happy to help them find the right person for the job. While I didn't get a big paycheck that month, I got something better—peace of mind.

—Anne, mom to Champ, five, and Hays, nineteen months

I walked away from my life as a music business executive for a more balanced existence. I created a career that supported that, but my thinking about self-care and time were still driven by the corporate machine. After my involvement in my PRG, I realized that I had to come first, even before my daughter. I began to see that the life I desired was possible. It all begins within me, and balance follows. Don't get me wrong, that perfectionist is still inside me, but I am so much more willing to look at my motivation and my deepest desires before I commit to things. The greatest gift I have learned in the last year is that saying "no" brings abundance. The more I say no to opportunities that don't feed my desire for balance, the more opportunities that support me make themselves available.

I feel like I have reached deep down inside myself and found a nice warm spot to reside. Much of the worry I used to have about life has lessened; I have started taking the time to truly appreciate the gifts I offer my family. Tapping into "me" through self-care has been a blessing.

—Wendy, mom to Ruby, six

month five

Good Is Good Enough:
A Mother's Mantra

For peace of mind, we need to resign as general manager of the universe.

—Larry Eisenberg, actor

Raising loving, emotionally healthy children takes a tremendous amount of energy on all levels—physical, mental, emotional and spiritual— particularly when our children are very young. This can leave us with a limited amount of time, energy and resources to devote to other areas of our lives.

Shortly after having my son, I realized that my expectations of having a clean house, serving healthy, home-cooked meals, managing my career coaching business, nurturing my relationship with my husband and being my son's primary caregiver were simply unrealistic. They would require more energy than I had available (even with a very involved and supportive partner).

Something had to give; I couldn't continue to operate in my "business as usual" fashion.

Yosemite National Park – Sierra Nevada, California

As background, throughout my twenties and into my early thirties, I was overburdened in my career with perfectionism and the need to feel in control. I was constantly raising the bar one more notch for myself. If I secured media coverage for a new PR client on the front page of the *Dallas Morning News*, I barely paused before I started pushing for a story in *People* or *The Wall Street Journal*. Ambition isn't bad, but the pressure I put on myself was not physically or emotionally healthy.

I was stressed out most of the time, anxious, overly focused on what others thought of me and never satisfied with my results. I felt nothing I did was ever quite good enough.

I slowly came to realize that the kindest self-care action I could take was to release critical thoughts and judgments about myself.

The beauty of focusing on your self-care practice is that you'll start receiving all kinds of side benefits. For me, one of these benefits was the realization that my perfectionist approach was the root cause of most of the stress in my life. No one around me was asking for more from me—it was all coming from the demands I was placing on myself!

I slowly came to realize that the kindest self-care action I could take was to release critical thoughts and judgments about myself. And relax about my expectations, particularly those around parenting and motherhood.

When my friend Andrea shared with her mother-in-law, Sally, what she was working on in her Personal Renewal Group—taking time for self-renewal and reconnecting with her desires and needs—Sally's eyes welled up with tears. She told Andrea, "I wish I had taken time for myself when I was raising my boys. Honestly, I just felt so overwhelmed by all the expectations I placed on myself during that time, it was hard for me to focus on much else. Because of all that, a lot of the time I was depressed and unhappy."

In that first year after Jonah's birth, I changed the way I approached a lot of things, including implementing a creative, flexible work schedule, limiting volunteer involvement, only spending time with friends who fed me emotionally and spiritually and eliminating a lot of extracurricular activities. But, more than anything, I changed my attitude from *I want everything to be the best it can be* to the healthier and much more human mantra, *good is good enough*.

And for the first time, I really started enjoying the things in life that were most important to me.

When we explore this theme in our Personal Renewal Groups, it's always a favorite topic. "'Good is good enough' gave me the freedom not to be so obsessive about whether my house was clean or not," shared Paula. Nina said, "Releasing the need for everything to be perfect gave me the freedom to have friends over, but with ease—hosting themed potluck dinners or informal pizza parties. I'll never cook a five-course dinner again."

Part of being able to relax into the mentality of "good is good enough" is understanding where your priorities lie. We have a finite amount of energy to devote to what's really important to us. If your relationships need extra nurturing or your child is going through a period in which he or she needs additional emotional support, you may need to live with a messy house, decline invitations to take on volunteer/work assignments or eat frozen dinners or scrambled eggs for dinner. Or if you choose to bring dinner to a new mother and her family, they may get a store-bought roasted chicken and "salad in a bag" rather than a homemade meal. And that's more than okay.

It was "good is good enough" that allowed me to actually complete this book! In the pre-baby days, I would have obsessed over irrelevant details that kept me from moving the project forward. When I wrote the *Guide*,

I was most concerned with getting the material and resources in the hands of other moms so they could use it to start their own Personal Renewal Groups. If I hadn't been able to relax into the "good is good enough" mentality, this *Guide* might never have made it into your hands!

A therapist once told me, "Your emotional well-being is of paramount importance; nothing else is more important. What are you willing to do to preserve this?"

Would you rather continually strive for perfection and feel like you're a slave to your to-do list or have your child remember moments when you dropped the vacuum cleaner to come and read her favorite story to her *one more time*? Or stopped working on the computer to go outside and watch the thunderstorm roll in and observe the green lizard on the window screen?

> "Your emotional well-being is of paramount importance; nothing else is more important. What are you willing to do to preserve this?"

One of my favorite quotes pretty much sums it up: "Life is not a business to be managed, it's a mystery to be lived."

The next time you begin something new or feel like you're in the center ring juggling more balls than you can handle, pause. It's completely up to you as to *how* you approach your task or commitment. No one's asking you to be Martha Stewart, and trying to accomplish tasks as a perfectionist typically means your self-care or your family's well-being may suffer.

When you're a parent and have children who need a lot of your energy, a "good is good enough" approach is often just the mantra you need to maintain your sanity and sense of well-being. The popular Southern saying sums it up: "If Mama ain't happy, ain't nobody happy!"

GUIDED JOURNALING EXERCISE:
Exploring "Good Is Good Enough"

*Set aside twenty minutes of quiet time to work on the exercise below
and then share your answers with your partner or a friend.*

What are three simple steps you can take to begin to implement
"good is good enough" thinking in your own life?

(1)

(2)

(3)

What personal beliefs or obstacles could keep you from practicing
a "good is good enough" approach in your life?

How does your vision of yourself as a parent now differ from the vision you had when you were pregnant? Why types of expectations did you have about being a parent?

How does the way your mother raised you or managed her household affect your perspective of how you want to parent?

In regards to how you parent, what are some of the things you should be patting yourself on the back for? Take a moment to celebrate those things you do really well.

"Shoulds" can get a lot of us in trouble. What "shoulds" come up for you around parenting or motherhood? Name three, observing how embedded some of these subconscious beliefs can be.

(1) Parents should . . .

(2) Mothers should . . .

(3) Fathers should . . .

TAKE ACTION:
Start Practicing "Good Is Good Enough"

During the coming month, apply the "good is good enough" approach to at least two significant projects, events or scenarios in your life that have the potential to be stressful (for example, birthday parties, volunteer assignments or family gatherings).

Notice if you feel differently before and after the activity when approaching it from a more relaxed perspective.

I hosted my six siblings for a family dinner on a Friday evening. I had originally planned to cook a big Mexican feast. The week leading up to our dinner was an unusually stressful one for me, and at the last minute, I decided to order Thai take-out. We put on great music, lit candles and served fun beverages. I was relaxed and grateful I decided to adopt the "good is good enough" mantra for this gathering. Not only did it end up being less work, but I was happier and calmer than I would have been otherwise!

Often when we hear the term *self-care*, we immediately think about ways to nurture ourselves physically. Actually, one of the most powerful ways to practice self-care is to start eliminating and releasing critical or judgmental thoughts about ourselves. Whether these thoughts come from feelings of inadequacy, a need to be perfect or a concern about what others think, they can have a huge impact on how you feel about yourself, how you interact in relationships and how you parent.

Over the next week, notice when and how often these critical thoughts pop up. Then identify one frequent negative thought or theme and try replacing it with an empowering one. For example, if you have negative self-talk about how disorganized you are, try replacing this thought with *I manage my life with ease and experience an abundance of time and support.* Try it; affirmations like these may feel hokey if you've never done them, but our behavior stems from our thinking. You've heard the saying, "change your thinking and you can change the world." It's true!

RECOMMENDED RESOURCES

Visit www.flylady.net to join an online support community or get tips and resources for household and life management

Confessions of a Slacker Mom, by Muffy Mead-Ferro

Self Matters: Creating Your Life from the Inside Out, by Phillip C. McGraw

Simple Abundance: A Daybook of Comfort and Joy, by Sarah Ban Breathnach

Stand Up for Your Life: A Practical Step-by-Step Plan to Build Inner Confidence and Personal Power, by Cheryl Richardson (www.cherylrichardson.com)

REFLECTIONS ON
"Good Is Good Enough"

Use this space to expand on your thoughts and feelings around this topic. See "Tips on Journaling" at the end of the *Guide* for support if you're new to journaling.

THE POWER OF SELF-CARE

I used to become physically sick from stress I put on myself to be perfect. If the laundry wasn't done or the house picked up, how could we leave to go to the park? And yet, if the kids didn't get outside, they'd drive me crazy. I'd react to their behavior by yelling at them. I was certainly far from perfect. Since I've starting thinking about what's most important to me in life—right now—I'm gaining better perspective. I have let go of a lot of things that I used to think mattered (a perfectly clean house). I also started to make my needs a priority, and now we have a much more harmonious household. Best of all, I appreciate and enjoy my children more than ever before.

—Megan, mom to Sarah, five, Will, three, and Thomas, eight months

I've learned that creating balance isn't just about saying "no" more often. In evaluating my workload and my kindergartener's potential after-school activities for the fall, I began to dread how busy we would become and that we'd have less time with each other. Even though we usually don't schedule more than one after-school program each semester for my daughter, the coordination of pick-ups and drop-offs, along with the nap and sitting schedule for my nine-month-old, can be a logistical mess. I am self-employed, and with many new clients calling to start Web site projects, I felt like I would have neither downtime with my daughters nor quiet space in my head.

So I said no to work. I remembered that I hadn't started my business to let it run me; I wanted to be my own boss and control my schedule. I gradually cut the number of projects I took on by more than a third, and I also said "yes" to something new—becoming a Girl Scout troop leader for my daughter's troop. My mom led my troop, and I had always envisioned being a troop leader some day. So now I'm looking forward to spending more time with my daughters and doing the kinds of things that I wanted to do as a mother. Sometimes saying no lets you say yes to creating space in your life for things that are really important to you.

—Amy, mom to Hannah, five, and Stella, nine months

month six

Let Your Light Shine:
Owning Your Personal Power

Our deepest fear is not that we are inadequate.
Our deepest fear is that we are powerful beyond measure.
It is our light, not our darkness, that most frightens us.
We ask ourselves, who am I to be brilliant,
gorgeous, talented, fabulous?
Actually, who are you not to be?
You are a child of God.
Your playing small does not serve the world.
There is nothing enlightened about shrinking
so that other people won't feel insecure around you.
We are all meant to shine, as children do.
We were born to make manifest the glory of God that is within us.
It is not just in some of us; it is in everyone.
And as we let our own light shine, we unconsciously
give other people permission to do the same.
As we are liberated from our own fear,
our presence automatically liberates others.

—Excerpt from "A Return to Love" by Marianne Williamson

Ancient ruins at Ephesus, Western Turkey

Over the years, I've facilitated numerous women's groups focusing on self-renewal and the importance of taking time to nurture oneself.

After a few years, I found myself becoming increasingly frustrated around one core issue: why is that some of us understand the concept of self-care on an intellectual level, yet have such a hard time making our self-care a priority?

One summer evening, while facilitating a Personal Renewal Group for moms at an Austin hospital, we slowly unraveled this topic. Surrounded by a circle of about fifteen intelligent, diverse mothers of all ages, I posed the question, "What thoughts or beliefs keep you from practicing self-care?"

For most of us, our lack of self-acceptance or feelings that we're not good enough or not deserving keep us from fully embracing self-care.

I jotted down their answers on a flip chart: *not enough time in the day, too difficult to make time for it, don't want to be perceived as selfish, my mom didn't take time for self-care—why should I?, I feel too guilty when I take time for me, my family doesn't support me in doing this, I shouldn't need to take time for myself* and on and on.

After about an hour of exploring this question, we moved deeper into the process and finally landed on the core belief that keeps most of us from embracing this practice: *I'm not worth it.*

For most of us, our lack of self-acceptance or feelings that we're not good enough or not deserving keep us from fully embracing self-care.

Thinking about self-love may feel strange or narcissistic. It certainly wasn't something that was taught or discussed when most of us were growing up. But it is essential to feeling whole, confident and emotionally resilient. Without it, we aren't really in a place that enables and encourages us to give to others.

Author Louise Hay says, "If you're looking for more love, then you need to love yourself first."

Erin, a twenty-five-year-old woman I worked with on a career change, shared that she wasn't certain whether she really deserved to be completely happy. This belief was sabotaging her ability to make a career transition and fully embrace new opportunities. Until she released this old thinking, she was going to continue to stay stuck in her patterns and self-limiting behavior. We can all relate to this scenario.

What most people experience is this: as our ability to love ourselves expands, so do our courage and willingness to more fully express our potential. I call this expression of potential "owning your personal power."

As a career coach, I often meet clients who sometimes feel held back in their lives and careers due to insecurities, inadequacies or fears of how others will perceive them. (For some reason, this seems slightly more prevalent among women than men.)

A common demon is that if they speak their minds or achieve notable accomplishments, they worry their friends' reaction will be *who does she think she is?* They often fear that if they break away from the pack, they will be ostracized in some way. So they stay safe and play small, remaining on the little kids' jungle gym and never really learning all that they're capable of—rather than branching out to experience the big kids' play space.

I spoke to a group of ten- to thirteen-year-old girls at a young women's career conference. As I was waiting to go on stage in a large auditorium filled with three hundred girls, I overheard a small group of four talking about their day. One of the girls was really on fire about what she had learned, and it had inspired her to share her career dreams with the others. I could see her face quickly shift from a state of open excitement and joy to one of repression and withdrawal as the other girls subtly expressed their discomfort at seeing their young friend so clearly own and express her personal power. It's too bad that Self-Love 101 isn't required coursework for all junior high girls.

Personal power is about living your truth, aligning with your life purpose and expressing your authentic self. It's fully expressing your potential and being all that you were meant to be.

As women, we often dance around our power, jump in and out of our power circle or maybe dip a toe in our power pool—occasionally experiencing a moment of enlightenment but then retreating again to the safety of obscurity.

Here are some ways you can practice standing in your personal power:

- **Find your voice.** Sometimes we remain quiet when we disagree with what is being presented. Speak your mind and express how you really feel. Don't overexplain or justify your position. Find your voice and use it!

- **Make your self-care a priority.** This is one of the best and clearest ways to validate your self-worth and send a message to yourself that *you are worth this investment.* Nurture yourself physically, emotionally, spiritually and mentally.

- **Stop caring what others think.** (You'll be working on this your whole life.) Imagine who you would be or what you would do if you didn't care what others thought of you.

- **Become comfortable using your masculine and feminine strengths.** We all have both. Living powerfully comes from the ability to balance and draw on both energies—doing and being, thinking and feeling, etc.

- **Practice being more direct and more assertive in your communication with others.** Notice how people respond to the way you communicate. Do you feel good about how you state your needs and desires and communicate with others?

- **Break away from the pack.** Do something just for you—because you want to, not because your friends are doing it or because you think you should do it. If you'd rather go for a hike than go see a movie with the gang—listen to your own needs.

- **Let your light shine.** Most of us are more afraid of our own light than of our own shadow. Take a risk, let others see your talents and gifts. Express yourself! Don't hold back.

- **Become financially savvy.** Creating your own nest egg, managing a household or business budget and/or co-creating a financial plan with your partner can be very empowering. Most people find getting their financial house in order to be very liberating!

- **Stop settling.** What do you want? Pause. What do you really, really want? Stop settling. The more comfortable you become at owning your power, the clearer you'll become on what you truly desire. Then you can start living the life you want.

The month before I turned forty, I invited eight high school girlfriends to Austin for the weekend—three of us were turning forty the next month and the rest had their birthdays shortly after that. Although I hadn't seen many of these women in years, and a couple I talked with only on rare occasions, I felt we all had a special bond for having spent very formative years together during our late teens.

I planned a special "Fabulous Forty" dinner downtown for the group, and after drinks, I made a small presentation to each woman. Each friend received a different magical snow globe wand that empowered her to "create" her future, and I honored a quality I most remembered her radiating at age sixteen, such as compassion, creativity, playfulness or wisdom.

Afterward, we each went around the table and shared what we had thought at age sixteen that we would be like at age forty. It was amazing to hear how we had each chosen to express our talents and passions.

My friends seemed touched by the celebration. There is something really unique and special about gathering with women who knew you at sixteen. It was a rare opportunity to really celebrate one another's true essence and stand in the knowledge of who we had become.

GUIDED JOURNALING EXERCISE
What Does It Mean to Own Your Power?

Schedule a twenty-minute break to further explore this topic. Have your journal nearby to record any additional ideas or thoughts that come up around this topic. Share your answers with a friend or your partner.

What are some ways you "own" your personal power?

How do you feel when you are standing in your personal power?

Who or what in your life/support system encourages you to stand in your power?

Who are models in your life—friends, colleagues or mentors—who own their personal power, and what is it that you admire most about them?

What needs to happen for you to more fully stand in your power?

How will you know when you are there?

Pull out a picture of yourself as a young child that really captures your essence. What quality do you see in yourself as a child that is now diminished or no longer with you? Really look at the photo, study it. What trait or quality jumps out at you? What do you need to do to nurture that part of you back into light? Remember, joy, confidence, enthusiasm and curiosity are your birthright.

Renée, age 5

Tape this picture to the inside of your journal. Then, looking at the photo, write about this quality and list three things you'll commit to do to ignite this hidden or diminished attribute within you.

When you're done, tape up the photo and your list of action items in a place you'll see it every day this month (your bathroom mirror, next to your bed, on your computer, etc.).

My friend Beth saw "playfulness" in her sweet one-year-old self. She said this diminished greatly when she started caring for her alcoholic mom when she was in high school. She decided to create a colorful, special altar in a corner of her room to honor her innate playfulness. She put her baby photo there along with an orange Play-Doh elephant, some purple nail polish and some bubbles. Her goal is to do one thing every day to bring out or celebrate the playful part of herself. Slowly, day by day, we reclaim who we are.

Power

Power made me a coat. For a long time I
kept it in the back of my closet. I didn't like to
wear it much, but I always took good care of it.
When I first started wearing it again, it smelled
like mothballs. As I wore it more, it started fitting
better, and stopped smelling like mothballs.

I was afraid if I wore the coat too much
someone would want to take it or else I would
accidentally leave it in the dojo dressing room.
But it has my name on the label now, and it
doesn't really fit anyone else. When people ask
me where I found such a becoming garment, I
tell them about the tailor, Power, who knows
how to make a coat that you grow into. First
you must find the courage to approach him
and ask him to make your coat. Then, you
must find the patience inside yourself to
wear the coat until it fits.

Excerpt from *The Book of Qualities*
—J. Ruth Gendler

Rent the movie *Whale Rider*, curl up on your couch with a blanket and some popcorn and settle in for a moving experience. In 2004, thirteen-year-old Keisha Castle-Hughes, the film's star, became the youngest person ever to be nominated for an Academy Award in the Best Actress category. Her performance is a shining example of a young woman who owns her power and is completely committed to letting her light shine regardless of what those around her say. This movie is appropriate for kids seven (use your own judgment) and older and is a wonderful film for the whole family to watch. I have seen it many times, and every time I continue to be touched deeply by its profound message.

RECOMMENDED RESOURCES

Fearless Living, by Rhonda Britten (www.fearlessliving.org)

Succulent Wild Woman, by SARK (www.planetsark.com)

Feel the Fear and Do It Anyway, by Susan Jeffers (www.susanjeffers.com)

You Can Heal Your Life, by Louise L. Hay (www.louisehay.com)

The Secret of the Shadow: The Power of Owning Your Story, by Debbie Ford (www.debbieford.com)

REFLECTIONS ON
Owning Your Power and Self-Love

Use this space to expand on your thoughts and feelings around this topic. See "Tips on Journaling" at the end of the *Guide* for support if you're new to journaling.

THE POWER OF SELF-CARE

I have never been good at achieving balance in my life. I always threw myself into whatever phase of life or new challenge I found myself in: college, career, traveling, career again, boyfriend, wedding planning, house remodeling, etc. So motherhood became the next challenge to obsess about. I wanted to experience as much as I could and didn't want to miss anything. I wanted to drink it up and cherish each moment.

*After all, you can never get back the first years of your child's life, but you have the rest of your life to sleep, work, exercise, etc. When friends, family and mentors would advise me to take care of myself and my relationship with my husband, I could understand what they were saying on an intellectual level. My brain could rationalize and understand that self-care was important, but the work (from the Personal Renewal Group) helped me to know it in my **heart**. I really believe that if I take care of myself first, I will have more to give to my husband and children. It's important for me to set an example for my children so that they learn to take care of themselves, lead healthy, balanced lives and realize their fullest potential.*

—Renee, mom to Harper, four, and Zach, two

month seven

Unleashing Your Creativity

Whatever you can do, or dream you can, begin it. Boldness has genius, power, and magic in it.
—Johann Wolfgang von Goethe, poet/philosopher

Ellen, a thirty-eight-year-old advertising agency executive and mother of two girls, came to me as a career coaching client, seeking help in making a career change.

She shared that she felt depressed, stagnant at work and undervalued at her job. Every Sunday night she would feel nauseous as her thoughts raced to the approaching work week.

After Ellen talked more about her situation (she used to do a lot of creative visioning and brainstorming for clients; now she was managing day-to-day account activity), it became clear that a large part of her frustration was that she didn't have the opportunity to express herself creatively at work (a complaint I hear often, whether the client is an engineer, manager or human resources specialist).

Yucatán Peninsula, Mexico

My homework for Ellen, while she was contemplating her career change, was for her to start to do something that would feed her creatively—now. Painting, belly dancing, jewelry making, ballet, creative writing, acting classes—it didn't matter. My stipulations were just that she do something "just for Ellen" and just for the joy of it—without attachment to how skilled she was at the particular activity. I also encouraged her to choose something from her past, before she had children, that had fed her creativity.

One of the many gifts our children bring us is the opportunity to be playful and explore our creativity while simultaneously encouraging theirs.

I visited with her two months later and saw that the exercise had clearly made an impact.

She shared, "I had no idea that taking up painting again would have such a profound effect on how I viewed everything in my world. For the first time, I'm actually excited about what lies ahead for me on my career path, but most importantly, I no longer feel sick on Sunday evenings and actually feel like I've reclaimed a lot of the passion for life I used to have. It's like my creative well was dry, and I have filled it with water again." Who would have known?!

One of the many gifts our children bring us is the opportunity to be playful and explore our creativity while simultaneously encouraging theirs.

My friend Andrea, an art school grad and mother of two preschoolers, says her kids give her an excuse—or permission—to explore her creative side with them. They'll make castles or modern art sculptures out of sugar cubes or use household items to make jewelry. She says she often feels most connected to her children when they are creating something new together.

My neighbor Diane started a Saturday morning Creativity Session for Moms. Once a month, eight to ten moms gather at her house, sans kids, to work individually or collectively on their creative projects. Imagine a room filled with vibrant women catching up on the week's activities while sketching, scrapbooking, beading, painting, knitting or creating collages. What a wonderful gift they're giving to themselves and to their families, who benefit immeasurably from moms who place a high priority on creative expression!

One of the gifts I received from my own mom, an accomplished jazz and classical musician, was an appreciation for and love of many different types of music. My mother battled depression most of her life, but she always turned to music for comfort and inspiration (our house, invariably, was filled every afternoon before dinner with Phil Ochs, Bach's Brandenburg Concertos or old John Coltrane).

Reflecting on this memory one day, I became inspired to start "Mom and Me" dance parties. The idea is to have a small group of moms and kids get together at our house on occasional Friday afternoons (we have a creative play space in the front of our house that remains open and unfurnished) and ask each family to bring two of their favorite "non-kid" songs for the group to dance to. How fantastic to explore creative movement with our little ones while exposing them to Indian chants, Latin grooves, world beat music and Vivaldi!

Think of a time in your past when you felt most open to life, most passionate. For me, painting, drawing, singing, writing, dancing or creating something new made me feel I was tapping into my creative essence. Creativity and the process of being creative are different for each of us.

"I always felt inadequate in the creative arts," Bridget shared. "I was an accountant, and most of my time prior to having the twins had gone into starting and running my own business. After I had the kids, I realized that birthing my business was highly creative and that coming up with new ideas, new programs and new services was how I expressed my creativity. This realization gave me confidence to help my kids try different creative pursuits. Painting or playing the piano are only two ways to express your creativity. There are many others!"

As a mom, a great way to nurture or reconnect with who you are is to re-engage in a creative activity you haven't tried in a while (or start something new). Nothing makes us feel more vibrant than tapping into the creative flow. Don't worry about doing something well, just enjoy yourself without judgment. Do it for the sheer joy it brings you. If it's been a long time since you've explored a creative pursuit and you're having trouble remembering what it was that fuels your creative juices, ask a childhood friend or family member to help you remember your favorite things to do when you were ten. What activity caused you to lose track of all time?

For some of us, it may have been years since we've explored our creative side. For others, this is an entirely new pursuit. Try the following guided journaling exercise to help you reclaim or reconnect with this part of yourself.

GUIDED JOURNALING EXERCISE
Exploring Your Creative Side

Set aside twenty minutes and find a special spot (nearby coffeehouse, natural setting, your favorite chair) where you can completely relax without distraction. Answer the following questions and don't think too hard before you reply—let the answers flow through you and onto the paper.

I am most creative when _____

_____

_____

Some of the ways I express my creativity are _____

_____

Doing creative things makes me feel _____

One of the most creative things I have ever done is _____

_____

When I was thirteen, some of the ways I expressed my creativity were _____

_____

_____

One creative pursuit I've always wanted to try, but never have, is _____

_____

Some things that hold me back from expressing my creativity are _____

_____

If I dedicated a whole day to creative activities, here's what my day would look like: _____

_____

_____

Some simple ways I can start expressing my creativity right now include _____

_____

Expressing my creativity is important to me because _____

_____

If I had to identify one single creative pursuit, project or legacy I would like to leave behind, I'd say it was

_____

_____

Share highlights from the exercise above with your partner or a close friend (or with another mom in your PRG), and take extra care answering "simple ways I can start expressing my creativity right now include…"

What will your next creative pursuit be? Be daring, have fun and express yourself creatively just for the feeling it brings you—don't worry about how "good" you are. T.S. Eliot inspires and reminds us, "Only those who will risk going too far can possibly find out how far one can go."

Tessa, a career coaching client, has a background in project management. She came to me shortly after she had left her corporate job in order to spend more time with her three-year-old. In the interim, while exploring her next steps, she wrote a beautiful, inspirational song about Lance Armstrong, the Tour de France champion. What was most amazing was that she had no musical background and had never written or even played music before, yet she created a remarkable (and commercially viable) piece of recorded music. What courage to be able to trust in your own creative abilities to that degree! She truly is one of my heroes.

SELF-RENEWAL TIP FOR THE MONTH
Take a Walk in the Wild

Find a nearby nature preserve in your area (call your local or state parks and recreation department, visit their Web sites or call the Sierra Club in your area for recommendations). Arrange for a couple of hours of child care on a Saturday or Sunday morning. Wake up early and go on a solo nature walk. Pack a water bottle, your journal, a pen and a snack. Wear comfortable shoes and bring a hat, if needed. Have your walk be a meditative experience. Be still. Close your eyes. Listen: what do you hear? Take time to really soak up the sounds around you. Feel the ground beneath your feet, how your shoes feel against the earth. Notice the subtle scents and how the air feels against your face. Pick up a fallen leaf, flower or branch—notice how complex the colors are. Record your thoughts or observances. How do you feel being alone outdoors? Nature has a way of connecting us with our source; I've found it's often one of the most spiritual practices you can engage in.

RECOMMENDED RESOURCES

The Artist's Way, by Julia Cameron

Creating a Life Worth Living, by Carol Lloyd

Creative Companion: How to Free Your Creative Spirit, by SARK (www.planetsark.com)

Writing Down the Bones: Freeing the Writer Within, by Natalie Goldberg

Use this space to expand on your thoughts and feelings around this topic. See "Tips on Journaling" at the end of the *Guide* for support if you're new to journaling.

THE POWER OF SELF-CARE

Caring for young children is perhaps the most creative work there is. It was not, however, work that supported my mental fitness routine of creative expression: writing, drawing and painting. For me, there were lessons of wonder, of endurance, of the nimble changing of the definitions of success. And lessons of discovery, patience and the understanding that when no other metric makes sense, the most delicious sense of humor can emerge. But there was no time to paint. I experienced postpartum depression, and I actually became afraid of my paints, thinking that they would poison my children. I tucked them away. Personal writing also became distant, risky. Did I want to continue to create these repositories of thoughts? What did that desire say about my priorities? I entered a stripped-down existence, throwing out pretty much everything I thought was mine before the children. My Personal Renewal Group helped me return me to my heart— with a hopeful, playful set of new creative inclinations. I learned to love the awkward, hurried pencil sketch of my husband sleeping. I stationed pastels in the bathroom and tried to catch the children's gestures as they bathed. In my larger works, I became intrigued with the interplay among pigment, water, and the resisting forces of oil and wax. Something about the unpredictability of those materials mimicked the art of motherhood. I found deep pleasure in bringing that complicated emotional algorithm of motherhood to life with my hands on canvas. A triumph.

—Sharon, mom to Anna, five, and Noah, three

month eight

Outrageous Living:
Reclaiming Adventure in Your Life

> *Courage is not the absence of fear, but rather the judgment that something else is more important than the fear.*
>
> —Ambrose Redmoon, author/rock band manager

I remember reading about a parenting survey that asked adults, "What was the single most memorable experience of your childhood?"

Emily, thirty, shared that it was the time her mom woke her up in the middle of the night with a box of donuts and a blanket, telling her they were going outside to have a star party. A rare meteor shower was supposed to be visible in the night sky at three a.m. Emily said this out-of-the-ordinary experience had always stayed with her and instilled in her an appreciation for adventure and spontaneity. She says growing up with moments like this made a huge impact on how she views life.

Yosemite National Park – Sierra Nevada, California

Erin, forty-two, said it was the time she saw her typically shy mother try paragliding for the first time. She and her siblings were in elementary school and knew their mother had a fear of heights. The image of her mother flying free and high in the sky—her purple shirt blowing in the wind—stays etched on her mind even today.

I myself am a risk-taker and love going new places and experiencing new things. I attribute this largely to a father who constantly surprised us with outrageous ideas and mini-adventures. Whether it was making us all line dance at the local Greek festival, trying his latest recipe (fig and apricot whole wheat fried pies!), digging a private limestone cave for my siblings and me in our backyard, surprising my mom with a box of Valentines' chocolates the size of a small country (much to our delight!) or taking us out to the Texas Hill Country to experience Fourth of July fireworks Peterson style (meaning he bought one of everything), my dad truly embraced his adventurous side, and his gusto for life was contagious.

Experiencing and embracing our adventurous selves—whether that means skydiving or trying a Vietnamese restaurant—is a marvelous way to reconnect with and nurture our essence. Often, when we have kids, we think we're supposed to act "parental" and squelch our desire to try new things. Where did we get that?!

Pushing ourselves a little outside of our comfort zones can be healthy and invigorating.

I attended a weekend coaching conference in Scottsdale, Arizona with a friend. I had scheduled a "me day" at the end of the conference and was looking forward to some downtime. I started driving around the area, dressed for an outdoor walk, but with no itinerary in mind. When

I saw signs for Camelback Mountain, I pulled over and parked in the recreation area at the base of the hills. Without reading signs or paying much attention to my surroundings, I started hiking up the winding, red dirt path (it was a Monday, so the trails were mostly empty). An hour and a half later, clinging to the side of a granite mountain face, scaling up a dramatic incline, I realized this was a serious climb. (A fellow climber equipped with major climbing gear told me it was a level five climb, on a scale of one to five!) Thoughts sped through my mind: *Is this safe? I can't do this—I'm a mom! Am I strong enough to finish this hike? What have I gotten myself into?!*

While holding onto the rocks with my bare hands and looking for places to put my feet (trying not to look down at the hundred-foot drop below), something within me ignited. I felt a burst of energy and confidence and pushed forward. Two hours later (and two miles up), I reached the top of the mountain. As I sat on the red rock enjoying the beautiful vista, I savored the feeling of sweat running down my back and a cool wind on my face. I felt incredible and more alive than I had in a long time! I have a piece of rock from the top of that mountain sitting on my bathroom counter as a reminder of my adventure. I see it every morning.

Trying new things, taking the less-traveled path or doing something out of the ordinary is very rewarding and can:

- make you feel alive

- open up your mind to what is possible (personally and professionally)

- breathe new life into relationships

- help you have a shift or see things in a new way

- remind you of who you really are

- inspire your children and friends to try living outside of their comfort zones

What is one thing you have always wanted to try but never have?

Many mom friends share that taking a trip alone is one thing they've always wanted to do. Those who have done it say it can be completely life changing, or at the very least, give you a new outlook on life. I try to take one solo trip a year (usually to a retreat center or a personal growth workshop in a beautiful natural setting), and every time I do, I'm reminded of how powerful it is just to be with yourself and get reacquainted with your hopes, dreams, fears and desires.

Others share they've always wanted to take up music lessons, learn how to grow vegetables, go back to school, complete a triathlon, go rock climbing, learn how to speak Spanish or French, write a children's book or swim with the dolphins.

I had a wonderful boss years ago when I headed up the marketing and tourism group at the state agency for historic preservation. The head of the agency was an archeologist and had a passion for learning and exploring that was unlike anything I've ever encountered. He told me one afternoon (he was sixty-two at the time) that he had a list of things he planned to do before he died, including visiting polar bears at the North Pole, swimming under the full moon in Lake Louise and hiking the Camino de Santiago pilgrimage in Spain. One afternoon, he shared that he only had two more items left on his list of one hundred. He died three years later. I hope he was able to experience those last two goals before he passed.

I challenge you to explore and reconnect with your essence by spreading your wings and trying something new.

Here are some simple ways my friends and I have injected adventure, passion and spontaneity into our lives. I'm hoping this may inspire you to come up with your own ideas:

- Take a trip alone (try an afternoon drive in the country; an overnight stay at a campground, B&B or spa; or a culinary vacation in Mexico).

- Take part in a full-moon activity (most cities have full moon hikes in local wilderness preserves, full moon yoga classes, etc.).

- Attend a local music or cultural festival in your city or a neighboring town (e.g. Chinese New Year or Mediterranean Festival).

- Pack a picnic dinner and head to the park—on a weeknight!

- Go canoeing, kayaking or rent a paddleboat—experience life in slow motion!

- Take your family (or yourself) out for a banana split and order three different flavors!

- Go hear live music (check with your local symphony, hear summer concerts in the park, visit a local jazz or blues club or check your weekend entertainment section for listings on your favorite bands).

- Line up a sitter and meet your husband (or a friend) on a Friday evening at a bar for happy hour and appetizers.

- Gather a group of girlfriends and take a salsa dance class together.

- Go on a hot air balloon ride or rent a convertible for the weekend!

- Organize a group family camping trip to a local state park.

- Check out your university's informal, non-credit class schedule— take a class on massage therapy, creative writing, meditation or Indian cooking!

Schedule a twenty-minute break to further explore this topic. Have your journal nearby to record any additional ideas or thoughts that come up around this topic. Share your answers with a friend or your partner.

What did my parents teach me about taking risks and trying new things?

What do I want to teach my kids about living outside of their comfort zones?

If I were to celebrate one time when I really stepped outside of myself and tried something new, what would that be?

What is one thing I have always wanted to try but haven't? Why not?

How do I feel when I try something new (whether it be a new food, a sport, a creative activity or a skill)?

TAKE ACTION
Adventure Challenge

Spend a few minutes thinking of two ways you'd like to add more adventure to your life in the next three months (or pick from the list on page 105). Write these down, share them with a girlfriend and then follow up with each other in a month to find out where you are and how your lives have changed. (Marking your thirty-day follow-up "date" with a girlfriend on your calendar will help you remember to have this conversation.)

(1)

(2)

Set aside ten minutes in the early morning or evening for peace and quiet. Lie down in a comfortable space. Take some deep breaths. Be still for a few minutes, then ask your body, *how do you feel; what do you need?*

What comes up? Are you craving movement/exercise? More sleep or rest? Are you hydrated? How is your energy level? Your digestion? Are you depressed or anxious or have you been having mood swings? How are your menstrual cycles? How do your feet feel? Your teeth and gums? Think about your neck and shoulders—are they tight or relaxed? Mothering asks a lot of our bodies; carrying, lifting, cooking, sleep deprivation and rushed or skipped meals can take a major toll. (My chiropractor says he is amazed at what mothers' bodies go through!)

Take note of how you feel and make it a priority (today!) to address your physical needs. Do you need to get a massage or see a chiropractor? Make an appointment for a general check-up or for your annual Pap smear or mammogram? Get support for healthier eating that meets your body's needs (maybe easing off the sugar, starting a multivitamin or adding more green leafy veggies, protein or fiber to your diet)? Do you need new shoes (they're often the culprit when it comes to back or headaches)? More physical activity (walking with a neighbor is a great start)? Make it a priority to listen to and respond to your body each day for a week. The more you check in with how you're feeling, the more attuned you'll become to your physical needs. And eventually, physical self-care will become more and more a part of your everyday routine.

Note: *I particularly love www.texasmedicinals.com. This mama-run company offers earth-centered, handmade organic herbal products for mothers and their families.*

RECOMMENDED RESOURCES

101 Things to Do Before You Die, by Richard Horne

1,000 Places to See Before You Die, by Patricia Schultz

Make Your Creative Dreams Real: A Plan for Procrastinators, Perfectionists, Busy People, and People Who Would Really Rather Sleep All Day, by SARK (www.planetsark.com)

REFLECTIONS ON
Reclaiming Adventure in Your Life

Use this space to expand on your thoughts and feelings around this topic. See "Tips on Journaling" at the end of the *Guide* for support if you're new to journaling.

THE POWER OF SELF-CARE

Learning to say "no" was a huge milestone for me. It improved my ability to manage my time, care for my family and care for myself. Magically, saying no increased the power and significance of saying "yes." Now, if I decline a coffee date, a project, a meeting, an event or a volunteer commitment, I do not feel guilty. I feel smart and in control. I feel more reliable. But I have to keep practicing. In my journal, I started a list of things that I decided not to do or declined. I'm more confident in my ability to make good decisions. I honor my family, myself and my time by saying no. And the rewards of that are so great. When I say no to many big and little things, I get to say yes to a few, very important things, beyond my family. I now have a leadership role in a local professional group. I have budding new friendships through my PRG. I am able to help clients whose work I love. I can usually whip out a dinner or an afternoon of babysitting for a friend with a new baby. I can spend a weekday at home with my daughters without checking email. For me, that is the power of self-care and learning to say no.

—Laura, mom to Megan, four, and Emily, two

month nine

Changing Relationships: Staying Connected

> To keep a lamp burning, we
> have to keep putting oil in it.
>
> —Mother Teresa

Having children can make two people feel closer than they could have ever imagined. It can also put strains on a marriage—and other key relationships—that can cause that sense of closeness to radically change or even disintegrate.

While attending a workshop at a yoga retreat center in Massachusetts, I eavesdropped on a revealing conversation.

A mother, along with her three beautiful young girls, was visiting the center from New York. She was waiting outside a studio with her kids, preparing to go into a parent/child yoga class. An older gentleman was teasing one of the girls, asking her if she was married. Jokingly (but bitterly), the mother exclaimed, "Why would you say that? Does she look miserable?"

Cinque Terre Region, Italy

People around her laughed nervously, but you could hear a pin drop after the weight of her comment fully settled in.

Often, after having children, couples find they begin to feel disconnected. This feeling is usually more intense when your kids are young, but it can continue as they get older as well. The physical, emotional, mental and spiritual stress of parenting can be extremely taxing.

How easy it is to wake up one day, look at your partner and ask, "Who are you and how did we get to this point?"

While I was on a plane traveling back from a workshop, the woman next to me (a forty-five-year-old mom with two preteens) shared that she and her partner had become "two ships passing in the night." They had conflicting work schedules (he worked night shifts, she worked during the day), and consequently they never had time to be alone, or even talk. Between the kids' commitments and increased demands at work, she was very concerned as she saw the distance between her and her husband growing. He was angry, and she felt depressed and undervalued.

When all your attention goes to caring for your children, helping with schoolwork and attending to household demands, how easy it is to wake up one day, look at your partner and ask, "Who are you and how did we get to this point?"

My friend Camille, who has been married for sixteen years and has two kids, shared with me that she keeps a small photo album next to her bed with photos of herself and her partner in the early stages of their courtship and marriage. The album also includes pictures of her husband doing things he is passionate about: windsurfing, hiking and cooking. She says these visual cues help her remember why she chose him as her partner and helps her connect with him in a new way. She says relationship work is really challenging for her, so everything she can do to help maintain that connection is good.

What are some things you can do to help foster and nurture the connection between you and your partner?

Make your relationship a priority. Devote energy and time to the relationship. A marriage is a living, breathing organism. It needs time, space, love and attention to stay intact. If it's not on your radar or is not a priority, it will fall apart, just like anything that is neglected.

Schedule (and keep) regular dates. Ideally, have a "date" with your partner at least every two weeks. Three to four hours of time for the two of you to connect, talk and just be alone together. You can have some of your dates at home in the evening if you can't get a sitter, but I recommend you ban any conversation having to do with kids or money. Also, save movie watching for another night, since it keeps you from engaging in conversation.

Nurture yourself first, so you feel like giving to your partner. If neither of you is making your self-care a priority, you won't feel like nurturing the relationship. Schedule alone time for self-renewal just like you would schedule a doctor's appointment. Then you'll be able to fully enjoy and be more present during your time alone together.

Touch each other every day. Hugs and kisses in the morning and at the end of the day, quick neck or shoulder massages, gentle arm touches and holding hands are all thoughtful and easy ways to stay physically and emotionally connected to your partner.

Create a bedroom that celebrates your marriage. A feng shui consultant once asked me, "Why do you have all these pictures of single women up in your bedroom? Where are the pictures of you and your husband?" Great point. Hang up pictures and place mementos of the two of you in your bedroom: special photos, candles, your intention statement (see page 117-118) or anything else that celebrates your partnership. Some people even create "marriage altars" in their bedrooms for these special things. Try to have your bedroom be a "toy-free" zone; make it a space for relaxation and connection.

Get your financial house in order (or at least discuss it!). The top two reasons couples fight stem from issues around money and communication. Make a commitment to have monthly discussions about finances, create a budget, address your debt, decide who will pay bills each month, meet with a financial planner or coach or find a way to come to peace with your money issues. Everyone has them. Decide how and when you and your partner are going to address yours in a way that best supports your relationship.

Get support, sooner than later. Don't wait until things get really bad to get the support of a therapist or relationship coach. Visit www.imagotherapy.com to find an Imago therapist near you (a really effective dialogue-based therapy model), ask friends for referrals, or if your partner is unwilling to go to marriage counseling, go by yourself. Author Wayne Dyer says, "When *you* change the way you look at things, the things you look at change."

Develop some ground rules or learn some tools for communicating with your partner. Relationship work can be challenging, and many of us don't have strong models to follow. In my marriage, one of our reminders to each other is "do you want to be *right* or be *in relationship?*"

> One of our reminders to each other is "do you want to be *right* or be in *relationship?*"

I also often resort to "quiet breaks" when I feel like I've reached my limit and am about to blow. It's always better to go this route than to say things you may later regret. I also know that my partner shuts down and withdraws when my voice escalates, so I try to be mindful of that. One friend sits down with her partner every Sunday night and they have family planning meetings for

the upcoming week to ensure they're communicating and are on the same page. They find it helpful, too, to give one another a heads-up if one of them has a particularly challenging week ahead and may need some extra support and TLC.

Take turns stating your relationship needs. "Three things I need from our relationship are..." Simple but powerful. Your needs will change depending on the time of the year, your life stage and kids' ages.

Connect every day for at least ten minutes. At the end of each day, share your high and low moment of the day. (See the exercise on page 122.)

Go away alone together for the weekend or at least for twenty-four hours. Have a family member help out or swap child care with a mom friend. You can stay in town at a hotel or visit a nearby bed and breakfast. I am always amazed by how powerful it is to be alone with your partner in a new environment. I have had friends who were on the brink of separation return from weekend trips and share that the getaway helped them see their partner and relationship in a whole new light. They felt reconnected.

Write an intention statement for your partnership. This can be a powerful way to communicate what you want your relationship to represent. Frame your statement and place it in your bedroom in a visible spot. See the next page for a sample statement.

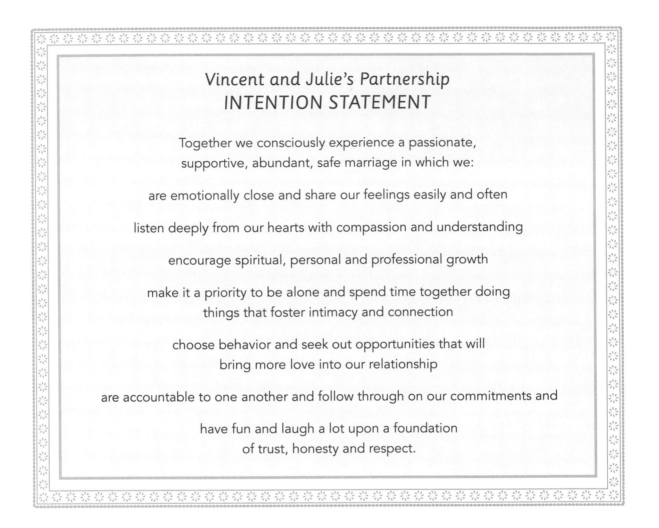

Vincent and Julie's Partnership
INTENTION STATEMENT

Together we consciously experience a passionate,
supportive, abundant, safe marriage in which we:

are emotionally close and share our feelings easily and often

listen deeply from our hearts with compassion and understanding

encourage spiritual, personal and professional growth

make it a priority to be alone and spend time together doing
things that foster intimacy and connection

choose behavior and seek out opportunities that will
bring more love into our relationship

are accountable to one another and follow through on our commitments and

have fun and laugh a lot upon a foundation
of trust, honesty and respect.

As a small girl, I remember feeling an incredible warmth and sense of security spread through my limbs whenever I saw my dad come up behind my mom while she was in the kitchen cooking, wrap his arms around her and kiss her neck and cheeks.

Being close and connected is not only healthy for your and your partner's overall well-being, it's integral to your child's as well. Most of what we learn about relationships we learned from our parents. Watch your child's face the next time you and your husband have a loving exchange—this is a teaching opportunity and they're taking notes!

Other relationships in your life change dramatically after having kids as well.

Relationships with your parents, siblings, grandparents, extended family, friends and even neighbors are also affected by this new life change.

"My brother and I are closer than ever because he understands how crucial family support is for parents," shares Colleen. "Both our parents have passed, but we're able to be there for each other now and take turns watching each other's kids. When I was single, we rarely saw each other or even talked; now it's almost every weekend."

Some women find that having a baby brings them closer to their family, while others say it distances them, depending on their family dynamics. Either way, there's no doubt about it: kids are little catalysts for everyone's personal growth when it comes to family relationships.

Most of us also find that friendships are more important than ever after you become a parent.

Often moms share that they don't have as much in common with their childless girlfriends once they become mothers. While I understand this sentiment, I find that some of my dearest friendships are with women who aren't moms. They help remind me of my various roles outside of motherhood and reflect back the "pre-baby" me. I work hard to maintain these special friendships as well as the ones with my mom friends.

New friendships become crucial, too. My friend Nancy shared that in her pre-baby life, she could never imagine being friends with some of the women she now hangs out with on a daily basis—they just wouldn't have had much in common. But now that they all have playful fourteen-month-olds who are sharing exciting, developmental milestones, these women have become her closest confidants.

My friend Erin says she constantly finds herself befriending other moms at the grocery store, park and in malls whose toddlers look to be the same age as her son, Noah.

The bond of parenting is strong.

Pause for a minute. Look at which friends and family members you used to see on a regular monthly basis, prior to becoming a parent. Now look at who you spend time with each month.

Becoming a parent will have an effect on all the key relationships in your life. Be open to letting your relationships evolve: making new friends, letting old friendships morph, reaching out to connect with family in new ways, stretching and getting involved with new circles of friends and finding new ways to connect with your partner.

It all goes back to the question: *what relationships feed me (and which ones drain me), and what do I need to feel nurtured and supported to live my best life?*

GUIDED JOURNALING EXERCISE
Exploring Changing Relationships

Schedule a twenty-minute break to further explore this topic. Have your journal nearby to record any additional ideas or thoughts that come up around this topic. Share your answers with a friend or your partner.

Which friends and family members really support, nurture and feed me?

Are there any relationships in my life that are draining me that I need to reevaluate?

When I'm having a rough time and need support, who are the first people I think to call?

Who are friends (and families) with whom my partner and I both enjoy spending time?
Is it important to us to have other families (and couples) we are able to connect with?

For one week, take five to ten minutes at the end of each day to connect with your partner by doing the following exercise. Find a quiet moment, either while the kids are playing or after they go to bed, pour a nice beverage and find a cozy corner to be together. *Take turns sharing (pick one to two questions to answer each night):*

What was the highlight of your day?

What did you learn today (professionally or personally)?

What made you sad or frustrated today?

What was the most meaningful thing you experienced today?

Your partner's answers may surprise you, but most importantly, you'll each have a sense of what is on the other person's radar—outside of day-to-day work and parenting demands.

Often when couples go on dates, they end up at the movies or some other type of activity that's fun but doesn't really give them the chance to deeply connect with one another. Purchase an interactive book of questions like *Love Tune-Ups* that provides you and your partner with opportunities for sharing and connecting (see the list below for suggestions). Set up a date at home in advance. Light some candles, enjoy a fire in your fireplace, open a bottle of wine or sparkling cider, order take-out or pop some popcorn. Then take turns playing with some of these questions and exercises. Really take time to enjoy one another's company. This is not the time to problem-solve or talk about household finances or what your coming week looks like. Your only job is to really listen to your partner and to emotionally connect. If you're having a hard time getting started, you might each take turns sharing "three things that attracted me to you were . . ." The date may feel stilted or funny at first, but give it some time. You are investing in your marriage. You'll be amazed what kind of returns you receive by making it a priority to consciously connect. Have fun!

RECOMMENDED RESOURCES

101 Things I Wish I Knew When I Got Married: Simple Lessons to Make Love Last, by Linda Bloom and Charlie Bloom (www.bloomwork.com)

Getting the Love You Want: A Guide for Couples, by Harville Hendrix (www.imagorelationships.org)

Three great "exercise" books for date night: *Love Tune-Ups: 52 Fun Ways to Open Your Heart and Make Sparks Fly*, by Matthew McKay, Carole Honeychurch, and Angela Watrous; *The Book of Questions*, by Gregory Stock; and *If . . . : Questions for Parents*, by Evelyn Mcfarlane and James Saywell

RECOMMENDED RESOURCES (CONTINUED)

Mars and Venus in the Bedroom: A Guide to Lasting Romance and Passion, by John Gray

Get a Financial Life: Personal Finance in Your Twenties and Thirties, by Beth Kobliner

The 9 Steps to Financial Freedom: Practical and Spiritual Steps So You Can Stop Worrying and *The Courage to Be Rich: Creating a Life of Material and Spiritual Abundance*, by Suze Orman (www.suzeorman.com)

Everything You Know About Love and Sex Is Wrong, by Pepper Schwartz

Spiritual Divorce, by Debbie Ford (www.debbieford.com)

REFLECTIONS ON
Changing Relationships

Use this space to expand on your thoughts and feelings around this topic. See "Tips on Journaling" at the end of the *Guide* for support if you're new to journaling.

THE POWER OF SELF-CARE

I have always felt like I needed to do my personal best at everything I do, because I have to fulfill my potential and the expectations of others. At first I thought it was "nurture"— maybe my parents' standards were too high, they did not give enough praise or I was feeling pressure as the oldest child. Then I leaned more toward "nature"—maybe I was just born with this perfectionist drive and need to please. And then one night in PRG, I had my lightbulb moment. I discovered that doing many things well or at least appearing to excel feeds my ego and supports my self-confidence. Also, the high of overachieving is addictive. I think I was defining myself and letting others perceive me solely through my deeds. More than a few people had jokingly called me "Martha" and that is not a good thing. My work in my PRG has been life-changing. It's helped me hit the pause button and shift my perspective. I've had the opportunity to slow down enough to think about things I would never have thought of before.

—Misty, mom to Ian, five, and Eliot, two

month ten

Motherhood as a Spiritual Journey

The purpose of our lives is to give birth to the best which is within us.

—Marianne Williamson, author

*I*mmediately after Jonah was born, I couldn't stand for him to leave my side.

On our first night together in the hospital, I slept with this small seven-pound wonder lying on a pillow on my sore belly (after twenty-four hours of laboring with a midwife, I ended up having a surprise C-section). For the entire night, I kept my hand on his tiny heart—wanting the intense connection I felt with him in the womb to never end. I think a part of me felt a little sad knowing that the journey of pregnancy was over and another one (for which I felt totally unprepared) was just beginning.

Something about feeling his tiny heartbeat against my palm stirred up a deep, primal connection to all the mothers and babies who had come before me. That first night with him was one of the most intense experiences I've had in my life. (Many of my close friends have shared that they didn't bond with their babies until they were older infants; I recognize and honor that the "mom meets baby" experience is vastly different for all of us.)

The light, love and strong sense of self that he exuded made me want to find and radiate that same love and light to others.

In those early months after my son was born, I rode a wave of emotions and had a strong sense that I would never view myself or my world the same way again.

Why are we here? I wondered. *Where or what exactly is God?* Other questions, like *what is my life purpose and how can I best express my calling?* took on new meaning and a greater sense of urgency.

My client Susan said that after having her second daughter, Emma, it became crystal clear that if she was going to work, she needed to do something that was completely aligned with her values and enhanced her quality of life. She not only wanted to be a role model for her young daughters, she also wanted her time away from them to be meaningful and worthwhile.

At times I experienced such incredible joy looking at my child that I momentarily understood why some women felt compelled to do this again and again. Jonah made me want to be a better person; he inspired me to want to challenge myself and grow on all levels—professionally, spiritually, emotionally and intellectually. The light, love and strong sense of self that he exuded made me want to find and radiate that same love and light to others.

My good friend Elizabeth said that after having their son, Ian, she and her husband felt an immediate need to find and cultivate their relationship with a spiritual community. For them, having a baby spurred a desire to deepen and expand their own connection to Spirit.

These feelings are quite common with many couples after they have a child. Many parents also find the first year after their baby is born to be a time of great soul-searching and reflection on their own spiritual education and upbringing.

Some new parents who never stepped foot in a church are eager to find a community to join. Others, who had less than positive experiences with organized religion, look to nature and healing environments to help nurture their child's spirit.

Maya, mom to five-year-old twins, shares, "The other day my son Ethan very assuredly told me, 'Mom, I think we need to find a church to go to today. I have something I need to say to God, and Bode [his classmate] said if I want to talk to God, I have to go to church.'" What great opportunities our little ones offer us to help them explore not only their divine nature, but ours as well.

I believe our children are our teachers.

My friend Camille said it's as if her daughter, Elian, holds up a "metaphorical mirror" to her mom's face every day, whether she's in the mood for self-exploration or not! It seems whatever you need to work on to further your spiritual growth—patience, compassion, self-love, gratitude, acceptance—your child will make sure you have the opportunity to explore that part of yourself.

No matter where we are on our spiritual path, having a child accelerates our personal growth and provides us with numerous avenues for self-discovery and life learning.

The spiritual gifts I've received from motherhood have been profound. Some of them include:

- **An increased capacity to love.** You often hear parents comment on how their understanding of love and ability to love becomes deeper. It's true.

- **A deeper sense of empathy and compassion for others.** I remember looking at a gruff, tattoo-covered convenience store clerk one day and thinking, as Jonah cooed in his sling, *this man is someone's baby boy.*

- **Increased understanding and greater empathy for the challenges parents face.** Now, more than ever, I am particularly aware of single parents, low-income parents and parents of children with special needs.

- **Being able to live in the moment.** Not all the time, but more easily! There is nothing that brings you to the present like a toddler who wants to stop every two feet to look at caterpillars or blades of grass.

- **Reclaiming joy in life.** It's not something that can just be experienced now and again—it's something you can have every day if you choose. Just watch your baby's eyes light up when she sees you walk in the room or when you take her to see something new she's never laid eyes on before!

- **An ability to clearly see what's really important.** What are your real priorities? What's essential, what would be "nice to do" and what needs to fall off your list or wait until later?

- **A clearer sense of what is right and wrong—for my own moral compass.** I remember visiting a museum when Jonah was three years old. As we paid for our admission, the woman behind the counter said, "Oh, two-year-olds are free." I started to move ahead and didn't think much of it, when I realized she was talking about my son. Feeling the "angel of ethics" on my shoulder, I plunked two dollars down on the counter. "Actually, he just turned three," I said, smiling. My sense of integrity took on a whole new level of meaning when I became my son's teacher.

- **Finding your voice.** Find motivation by stating your child's needs to others (particularly if they're not able to speak yet). Many women claim they first found their voice after becoming mothers. Do you find it easier to speak your truth now than you did before having kids?

Regardless of your personal beliefs, spiritual self-care is essential to your overall well-being. It's about feeling centered, nurturing your essence, enhancing inner strength, living in integrity, trusting, experiencing a connection to a higher power, feeling a sense of purpose and finding meaning in your life.

GUIDED JOURNALING EXERCISE
Motherhood as a Spiritual Journey

Set aside some quiet time, light a candle, curl up in a blanket with your Guide and take a moment to reflect on your own spiritual/personal growth since your child(ren) were born.

What are some of the gifts you've received from motherhood?

(1)

(2)

(3)

How have these insights or life lessons influenced how you live or approach life?

How have they influenced your values, sense of personal integrity or ethics?

How has having a child affected how you view religion, spirituality or your perception of a higher power?

What has surprised you the most about becoming a mom?

How has becoming a mom affected the way you view yourself as a woman?
As a spiritual being?

If your child(ren) are your teachers, knowing what you do about their personalities,
what do you think they are here to teach you?

How has becoming a mom affected how you view your mother? Your father?

How has your concept of love changed since becoming a parent?

 TAKE ACTION
Facilitating a Dialogue

Share the questions above with your partner. After each of you has finished the exercise, set up a date (this can be as simple as sharing strawberry-peach smoothies after the kids go to bed one evening).

Discuss this chapter and take turns sharing your responses.

If you like, choose one to two action items that enhance your individual and family's spiritual growth that you both agree to follow through on (example: your partner wants to attend a weekend meditation retreat or you want to try out a new spiritual community you've been interested in visiting).

Initiate further dialogues around this topic as needed or consider hosting a supper circle with other parents who are also interested in discussing this theme. New parents in particular often find parenting gives them a lot of food for thought when it comes to exploring issues around spirituality.

SELF-RENEWAL TIP FOR THE MONTH
Going Inward

We live in a society where we are trained to rely greatly on external resources for answers. In fact, we each have within us a well of wisdom, insight and a knowingness about what is best for us in any circumstance (be it related to parenting, relationships, life direction, career, etc.).

Some people call this inner wisdom their intuition, some people call it their connection to God; either way, the secret to accessing this built-in guidance is to carve out time to be still and alone.

It would be ideal to have these mini-meditations on a regular basis, but if you're feeling crunched for time, start by having quiet moments in incremental doses. The next time your little one takes a nap or you have a morning or evening to yourself, take some deep breaths, light a candle and sit quietly. Let the day's challenges and excitement fall away. Close your eyes, take some deep breaths and just "be" for few minutes. Whether you call this prayer, mediation or just quiet time, realize it may take a while for all the chatter to fall away and for you to begin to tap into that expansive, peaceful feeling. That's okay. It takes practice. The more you do this, the more comfortable you'll get with it and the more easily you'll connect with that quiet inner voice. The sense of comfort and well-being you'll get from connecting with your Source is like no other.

RECOMMENDED RESOURCES

The Experience of God (stories from spiritual teachers around the world), edited by Jonathan Robinson

Inspiration: Your Ultimate Calling, by Wayne W. Dyer

A Return to Love, by Marianne Williamson (www.marianne.com)

Sabbath: Finding Rest, Renewal, and Delight in Our Busy Lives, by Wayne Muller

The Seat of the Soul, by Gary Zukav

Walk a labyrinth. To find a labyrinth near you, visit www.unity.org and click on "find a church." Your local Unity church can typically give you a list of area labyrinths.

Subscribe to www.dailyom.com to receive inspirational thoughts that nurture your body, mind and spirit.

REFLECTIONS ON
Motherhood as a Spiritual Journey

Use this space to expand on your thoughts and feelings around this topic. See "Tips on Journaling" at the end of the *Guide* for support if you're new to journaling.

_____

_____

_____

_____

_____

_____

_____

_____

THE POWER OF SELF-CARE

"Becoming a mother sent me on an inward journey and made me look beyond the here and now. Before having children, I was in a spiritual desert or void and lived only in the world of intellect and ego. When my older son Bryan was born with Down syndrome, he opened me up to a beautiful world of light and love. He and his younger brother woke me up to the truth of who I am and helped me reconnect with our Creator and remember my life purpose. My precious sons gently reminded me to make time to get quiet and listen to the still small voice inside of me that is our Source. These two special angels reunited me with the spark of divinity that is within all of us, and helped me discover the peace and unity found through a deep connection to Spirit."

—Rhonda, mom to Bryan, five, and Dylan, two

month eleven

Reclaim Your Life:
Strategies for Balance

Life is a marathon. You can have and be all the things you want to be. Just do it over a lifetime. Don't try to do them all at once, because you can't. If you try to, everyone around you will suffer—most of all, you.

—Eunice Kennedy Shriver, activist/philanthropist

Are you the master of your life or a slave to it?

Do you have enough time for those things in your life that are most important to you?

Ten years ago I was handling public/media relations for a large international biotech corporation. The culture was typical of most large companies: they expected long hours, work/life balance was never discussed and vacations were few and far between.

I had not had a vacation in two years when my girlfriend suggested we take a trip to Europe for two weeks. We were both single and I badly needed a break, so I jumped at the chance. At the last minute she had to cancel, so I signed up for an adventure tour and headed to Amsterdam alone to meet my group.

Ten days into the trip, we stopped in Munich and visited Dachau, the Nazi concentration camp. The experience was chilling, to say the least. As I walked through the barracks, I picked up mental postcards that remain etched in my mind, even today.

After the walking tour, I left the group and walked outside with my journal, settling under a large shady tree to write. I asked myself, *what is one word that encapsulates my experience at the concentration camp?* I wrote the word down in my journal.

As I finished, the image of my boss and my job in Austin flashed through my mind. Suddenly my body was wracked with nausea and I became sick. Reeling from the intense experience, I sat, stunned. What in the world did my PR job in Austin have to do with Dachau, and why was this connection making me ill?

I slowly looked down at my journal to the page where I had been writing. In huge block letters was the word *OPPRESSION*. I had made a visceral connection between how the prisoners must have felt at Dachau and how my current job made me feel. (I recognize there is no way to compare the two on an intellectual level—this was just my emotional response.)

My gut feeling was really trying to tell me something.

A week later, while flying back from Paris to Austin, I heard an interview on National Public Radio with a woman named Carol Orsborn, author of *Inner Excellence: Spiritual Principles to Life-Driven Business.* The day I got home, I bought her book, stayed up all night reading it, went in to work the next day and (to the great surprise of my director) quit my job.

I ended up taking a three-month sabbatical, and it became crystal clear that the time had come for me to reclaim my life and my sense of balance. The experience at Dachau had forever changed the way I looked at and managed my life.

I receive many requests to lead work/life balance workshops for companies and organizations; not surprisingly, the topic of how to experience more balance in your life is more popular than ever.

I believe we're at a very unique time in history.

The convergence of many factors—the 9/11 tragedy, an unstable economy and job market, a 24/7 digital culture that suffers from information overload, the need to "parent our parents" while parenting our children, heightened levels of multi-tasking (to the point of ineffectiveness)—have created a society that feels off-balance, out of synch with its own rhythms and needs and completely and utterly overworked and overwhelmed.

Whether your work involves caring full-time for your children, managing your own business or going to a workplace every day, these converging factors have and will continue to affect us all in profound and numerous ways.

How can you begin to reclaim your life and experience more balance on a day-to-day basis?

I have found it helpful to look at approaching and defining balance as having enough time, energy and resources for those things in life that are most important to you.

In my work with thousands of clients in the area of life balance, I have found it helpful to look at approaching and defining balance as having enough time, energy and resources for those things in life that are most important to you.

My approach to balanced living focuses on four core strategies *setting priorities and managing your energy, taking time for self-renewal, building a support network* and *being more present in your life.*

Picture yourself sitting comfortably on a beautiful, sea-blue, four-legged stool, which completely supports you in feeling more balance in your life. Each leg represents a different area, or strategy.

Here they are in a little more detail.

Strategies and Insights for Balanced Living

Know your top priorities and effectively manage your energy. What in life is most important to you? How good are you at managing your energy? What is draining you? What is fueling you? Are you comfortable saying no and not over-committing? Create a Top Life Priorities list and adhere to it! If it's not one of your top three priorities right now, it's going to have to wait.

Make your self-renewal a priority. By filling your cup first, you'll have more to give to family, work and creative projects and yourself! You'll be able to function at your optimum and set an example for healthy, balanced living for those around you. Self-care (on all levels—physical/mental/emotional/spiritual) is essential to balanced living.

Build a personal support system. What type of and how much personal and professional support do you need to feel nurtured, emotionally healthy and stress-free? Learn to ask for and receive help. Reevaluate your support needs every three months; these change based on your current life stage. Having a support system when going through a transition or stressful time can have a huge impact on how you experience the journey.

Be more present in all that you do. *(You'll explore this topic in greater detail in Month Twelve.)* Stress and overwhelm are often brought on by dwelling on the past or living in the future. By spending more time living in the present and focusing on what is most important here and now, you'll feel calmer and be more effective. In general, when we're living in the present, we experience a greater sense of balance and well-being. One specific way to be more present is to be mindful of how and when we use technology (cell phones, computers, PDAs, email/Internet and telephones). These tools have the tendency to overwork us!

When making changes, it's good to start with baby steps and be gentle with yourself.

The good news is that the *Guide* has already helped you practice strengthening each of these areas (if they're new to you, go back and read Months Two, Three and Four on self-care, building a support system and managing your energy).

Most importantly, realize that you're in the driver's seat when it comes to how you manage your career and life (even though it may feel at times like you're in the back seat or even the trunk!). When making changes, it's good to start with baby steps and *be gentle with yourself.*

I've found the following insights to be comforting and helpful when it comes to thinking about experiencing more balance in my life. Use these tips to help support you on your journey towards reclaiming your life.

Tips for Experiencing Greater Balance In Your Life

- Live with (and accept) the way things are rather than the way you think they should be. This can be helpful in how you experience life on a day-to-day basis. If it takes an hour to get to work in the morning in traffic, that's how long it takes. If you child needs fifteen minutes to say good-bye to you in the morning, create a schedule that accommodates that.

- Realize that there are days or weeks when you'll feel like you have a handle on things and other times when it feels like you're flying by the seat of your pants—know that this is all part of the journey of motherhood. *Breathe.*

- Pause often to reflect and ask, *what's really important here?* This will help you keep a healthy perspective on life and the curve balls it regularly throws.

- Remember that each of us only has a finite amount of energy to work with. In general, try to under-schedule, under-commit and under-promise when it comes to obligations. When you throw children into the mix, things *always* take more time and more energy than you think they will.

- Maintain your self-care strategies, particularly during weeks or periods when you know you have an unusually hectic schedule. Make time for exercise, have healthy/easy food on hand, get plenty of sleep, schedule short periods of downtime and ask friends and family ahead of time for extra support during this busy time. Also, ask yourself, *is everything I have planned for this week really necessary? What can I take off of my to-do list? What can I say no to? What can wait?*

- Make sure you're scheduling and keeping regular dates with your partner. Time to rejuvenate and have fun is essential to maintaining your sanity and sense of humor when juggling all of life's activities.

- Consider setting a personal and/or family intention for the week (e.g., "This week our family is open to experiencing fun and joy in new and unexpected ways."). This affirmation can help guide and ground you before you ease into the week's activities.

- Live in the present as much as possible. Planning is great and helpful, but if you can balance this with thinking only about what you have to do in the next moment, hour, etc.—not what has to be done by Friday or by next month—you won't feel so overwhelmed.

A mentor often kindly and gently reminds me that each of us is doing the best we can at any given time. And when we know better, we'll do better.

Pause and reflect. Are you directing your time, energy and resources to those things in your life that are *most* important to you? If not, it's a good time to get some support and make some changes.

GUIDED JOURNALING EXERCISE
Enhancing Balance in Your Life

Schedule a twenty-minute break to further explore this topic. Have your journal nearby to record any additional ideas or thoughts that come up around this topic. Share your answers with a friend or with your partner.

Based on the insights on the previous pages, what are three specific things you need to do to create more balance in your life today?

(1)

(2)

(3)

Are you clear on your Top Life Priorities (as outlined in chapter four)? Are you directing your energy and resources toward those areas?

What area of self-care (physical, mental, emotional, spiritual) do you need to focus on over the next three months? What specific things do you need to do to make your self-care a priority?

Do you have a robust support team? If not, what areas need to be enhanced?

How present are you in your day-to-day life? Do you need to reevaluate and tweak your daily routine so that you're not in a constant state of "monkey mind?"

Finally, if you were to adopt one mantra to help you feel more calm, effective and relaxed on a regular basis, what would that be?

 TAKE ACTION
Create a Vision Map

Note: *This is a great Personal Renewal Group activity*

As mothers, we're often in a constant state of *doing*. We forget that our attitude, perspective or intention behind how we accomplish tasks have a huge impact on our day-to-day life. Plan an evening date with a girlfriend. Gather some old magazines, scissors, tape and a large sheet of paper. Put on some relaxing, upbeat music. Create a vision map of how you want to *be* in the world. Start by coming up with a list of five to six adjectives (or more) that describe how you want to be, and choose photographs, drawings or images from magazines or postcards that represent these qualities for you. For example, some women might choose adjectives such as wise, compassionate, patient, trusting, assertive, open-minded, etc. When I chose "trusting" as how I want to be, I used a photo of a woman dressed in white standing at the edge of a cliff. Choose images that resonate with **you**, and when you're done tape up your collage somewhere that you can see it as a regular reminder of your intention for *how* you will approach what you do. This is a great exercise to remind us that *being* is just as important as *doing*.

Most of us don't enjoy the feeling of rushing from one thing to the next. What a treat it is to arrive somewhere early and have a few minutes to read or just relax! For the next month, try padding your schedule with a little extra time so you're not rushing to doctor's appointments, meetings, friends' houses, parties or the sitter/day care. Since having a child, I've found one way to reduce stress for our family is to overestimate the amount of time it will take to get somewhere. Often, when I mark down an appointment on my calendar, I'll make a mental note of what time we need to leave the house in order to travel and arrive at our destination with time to spare. It's amazing how nurturing an extra ten minutes of breathing space can feel and how it can impact your day, how you parent and how you interact with others. After doing this for a while, you start to make it a habit and the rushing (although it's bound to still happen occasionally) becomes a less-frequent occurrence.

RECOMMENDED RESOURCES

Finding Your Own North Star: Claiming the Life You Were Meant to Live, by Martha Beck (www.marthabeck.com)

Callings: Finding and Following an Authentic Life, by Gregg Michael Levoy

How to Find the Work You Love, by Laurence G. Boldt

The Path: Creating Your Mission Statement for Work and for Life, by Laurie Beth Jones

Life's Work: Confessions of an Unbalanced Mom, by Lisa Belkin

Living Your Best Life: Ten Strategies for Getting from Where You Are to Where You're Meant to Be, by Laura Berman Fortgang

Work Less, Make More: Stop Working So Hard and Create the Life You Really Want!, by Jennifer White

The Seed Handbook: The Feminine Way to Create Business, by Lynne Franks

Helpful Web sites for working moms: www.jobsandmoms.com, www.workoptions.com and www.superbusyparent.com.

REFLECTIONS ON
Creating Balance in Your Life

Use this space to expand on your thoughts and feelings around this topic. See "Tips on Journaling" at the end of the *Guide* for support if you're new to journaling.

THE POWER OF SELF-CARE

I learned that caring for yourself is not selfish, but rather a necessity of being a good friend, wife, mother and employee. I have much more to give the people in my life when I feel more in balance, rested and healthy. This requirement changes shape depending on the moment—it could mean taking time for a yoga class, going to dinner with girlfriends or taking a nap (instead of doing laundry) on the weekends. I am a recovering perfectionist and have learned that I can't do everything perfectly all of the time. I've become much more comfortable with the concept of focusing my time and energy so that one area of my life gets a lower or higher percentage of attention that week, day or even hour. It can't be split up evenly all of the time. And, it's your contribution over time, as a mother, wife, friend, employee, etc., that counts—one hour does not define your overall performance. My stress level and our family dynamic have improved infinitely as a result of my shifts in how I think, and this is the best gift I could have ever imagined.

—Tonja, mom to Annabelle, four, and Parker, twenty-one months

One of the biggest benefits I've received from my PRG experience has been the reminder to be gentle with myself and to pay close attention to how I manage my energy, as opposed to just managing my time. When I take a moment to step back and truly reflect on my schedule and what it will mean in terms of an energy commitment, I can pinpoint areas of my life that drain me or add too much stress. Shortly after I started PRG, my husband began to travel frequently for work. With the tools I'd been practicing from PRG, I was able to manage my time and energy while I was solo parenting in a way that kept me from becoming completely overwhelmed by the task of caring for our two kids, running my home-based business and taking care of myself. I worked breaks into my schedule, like lunches with girlfriends, while my husband was out of town. I made sure I had support lined up in the way of sitters and playdates, so I would actually have a chance for much-needed adult conversation! I tried to keep my schedule as light as possible during those weeks he was gone, and I really thought about how/where I was using my energy. As a result of my wise choices, I didn't get (as) frustrated or angry with the kids during challenging moments, I felt less resentment toward my husband's job and travel schedule and I was able to keep our lives running smoother and more in balance.

—Rachel, mom to Anna Kate, five, and Ben, two

month twelve

Being Present and Remembering What Really Matters

Don't die with your music still in you.

—Wayne Dyer, author/speaker

Thirty days before my wedding day, my mother died suddenly from congestive heart failure brought on by an unexpected case of the flu. She was healthy, active and sixty years old. The loss was unexpected and hit hard, following the sudden death of my father four years earlier and my brother four years before that.

I am a different person because of these losses. They say losing a parent has a life-changing effect on you. The change for me was and is in *how I see the world* and *who I decided to become in the world.*

I had a career client, Robert, whose brother had died the year before of cancer. It had prompted Robert to reevaluate his life direction and perspective. Another client, Emma, had survived a malignant brain tumor, and the experience had lit a fire under her to find and express her true life purpose.

Frio River – Concan, Texas

Most of us have, at some point, been touched by a life-changing event. It may have been a birth, a death, a divorce, an illness, a job loss, a

If real growth is to come from a major life transition, the question to ask yourself is *how has or will this experience change how I live and who I am in the world?*

financial challenge, an act of terrorism or a natural catastrophe. (My inbox and voice mail were flooded with calls from new clients after the 9/11 tragedy. The incident was an awakening to many to pursue the life and/or career they really wanted to be living.)

If real growth is to come from a major life transition, the question to ask yourself is *how has or will this experience change how I live and who I am in the world?*

For me, the premature loss of immediate family members left me with a sense of urgency and clarity about how important it is to really live the life *you want to live* and *the life you should be living.*

I love the question Stephen Levine addresses in his book, *A Year to Live: Living This Year As If It Were Your Last.* What if you knew this was your last year on the planet? How would that awareness change your perspective and the choices you make on a day-to-day basis?

Would you treat your spouse differently? Would your conversations with your friends change? Is there something you would take action on that you've been postponing until the time is right? Would you interact differently with your children?

When most people are asked the question "how would you live this day (or year) if you knew it were your last?" they respond that they would be *more present in their relationships and in all that they do.*

My son loves nothing more than to be out in nature exploring (something I loved to do as a kid with my brothers as well).

My friend Diane and I took our boys to a local state park. The sun warmed our backs and heads and the nearby waterfalls soothed our ears as we walked slowly over the rocks, following Jonah and Noah, letting them guide us to whatever natural treasure they happened to discover.

Our boys became mesmerized by the shells they found on the edge of the creek bed leading to the falls. We spent the next two hours there, sorting, exploring, feeling and collecting the beautiful shells.

While some of the stones look very similar to me, Jonah always points out the subtle differences between the color, size, texture and variation in his gems.

Walking along the creek, as I glanced at my watch and my mind rushed ahead to dinner plans and work emails I needed to return that night, my son looked up at me, smiling and holding out a beautiful purple shell in his small hand. "Mama, isn't this the mostest beautiful rock you've ever seen?" he said.

How often do we pause to be present and really enjoy the beauty of a moment or place? Will we be present enough to recognize these gifts when they're extended to us?

Being more present in our relationships—particularly with our partner and children—has huge benefits. When we're present with those around us, we're able to experience openness, connection, joy, playfulness, spontaneity, compassion, empathy, gratitude, wisdom and enhanced communication.

In *Slowing Down the Speed of Life*, author Richard Carlson shares that several serious consequences follow from busy-minded, speeded-up parenting. Some of them include:

~   You become habitually reactive instead of responsive.

~ You take negative behavior personally rather than seeing the innocence.

~ Little events become front-page news.

~ You miss the good times.

~ You lose sight of your compassion.

~ You expect too much from your children.

When I feel pulled between the demands/challenges of life *and* focused on how I can be more present in my everyday life, I find it helpful to pause—often—and ask the following questions:

- Am I living in the past, present or future? (If I'm feeling stressed, I'm either living in the past or the future. There is no stress in the present moment.)

- A year from now, will this really matter?

- In this moment, what is most important?

- Does this **really** have to get accomplished today (this month, this year)?

- What is my intention for the day? What kind of day do I want to have? (I ask my son this in the morning before preschool, helping him to begin to connect how his thoughts impact his experience and the kind of day he has.)

Finally, be gentle with yourself. We live in a 24/7 culture that is overly focused on multi-tasking and producing. Most of us were never taught that *being* is just as important as *doing*. Slow down. Take time to really soak up life.

I think most mothers will agree: we want to teach our kids that we value them for who they are, not for what they do.

Schedule a twenty-minute break to further explore this topic. Have your journal nearby to record any additional ideas or thoughts that come up around this topic. Share your answers with a friend or your partner.

How would I live this year if I knew it were my last?

When I'm very present with my child(ren), how does this affect how I parent?

Do I find myself living in the past, future or present most of the time?

I know I'm living in the "present" when I feel…[complete].

TAKE ACTION
Exploring What Matters Most to You in Life

Set aside twenty minutes for the following exercise. If you'd like additional writing space, you can use your journal to record your answers. Put on some uplifting music (e.g., Vivaldi's *Four Seasons*) while you work. This can be an intense exercise.

You have just learned you will never see your children again.

However, the child(ren) will receive a letter from your husband tomorrow about what was most important to you in life.

Close your eyes, take some deep breaths. Rise above your sadness, and with a sense of urgency, passion and purpose, reflect on what you most want your children to remember and know about you.

Begin the exercise using the guided letter on the next page.

_____(Today's date)_____

Dear_____(child's name)_____, I'd like to share with you a few things that were really important to Mom.

Mom was very passionate about _____

_____

Some of the things she loved to celebrate in life were _____

_____

Her favorite quote, book or author (and why) was _____

_____

She always made time for _____

_____

If she had a free day, she'd spend it _____

_____

Her motto or slogan for life was _____

_____

She loved to teach you about _____

_____

She sometimes got tears in her eyes when _____

_____

She got angry when _____

_____

She often volunteered her time to _____

_____

She most admired _____

It was important to your mom for you to know who she really was. I hope this letter helps you understand what an incredible, magnificent person she was, and how much of her will always live in you, too.

Love,
Dad

SELF-RENEWAL TIP FOR THE MONTH
Take a Gratitude Walk

Go for a short twenty-minute walk (alone or with your family) in your neighborhood or on a nearby greenbelt. Stretch a little and then raise your arms over your head a few times, breathing deeply and filling your body with oxygen. Start walking and observe your environment: the tall trees, the changing sky, animals, neighbors, your house, your community. Then slowly share aloud (and, if present, have your family members share) five things you're each grateful for. If this is easy, you can keep going and listing additional things. We do this a lot in my family when one or all of us is in a grumpy mood. (Either on a walk or just at the kitchen table before a meal.) It's amazing how moving into a state of gratitude can help shift a negative mindset or low mood. You can also take out your journal when you're feeling down and spend five minutes writing—nonstop—listing everything in life you're grateful for. If you find it hard to get started, begin with small things: a hot shower, chocolate chip cookies, clean sheets, green grass, etc.

RECOMMENDED RESOURCES

You Can Be Happy No Matter What: Five Principles Your Therapist Never Told You, by Richard Carlson

Loving What Is: Four Questions that Can Change Your Life, by Byron Katie and Stephen Mitchell (www.thework.com)

Slowing Down to the Speed of Life: How to Create a More Peaceful, Simpler Life from the Inside Out, by Richard Carlson and Joseph Bailey

The Power of Now: A Guide to Spiritual Enlightenment, by Eckhart Tolle

A Year to Live: How to Live This Year as if It Were Your Last, by Stephen Levine

Rent *What the Bleep Do We Know?* (www.whatthebleep.com) or *The Secret* (www.thesecret.tv), two documentary-style movies exploring the connection between what we think and how we experience life

Use this space to expand on your thoughts and feelings around this topic.
See "Tips on Journaling" at the end of the *Guide* for support if you're new to journaling.

THE POWER OF SELF-CARE

The road to making your self-care a priority can be a long one. But I have found it to be so rewarding and the key to unlocking joy in my life. My alcoholic mother passed away when I was eighteen. I recently went to lunch with an old friend of hers who brought me a picture of my mom as I had never seen her—relaxed and happy with my dad. My mom's friend challenged me to remember when I was a cherished newborn, before things, as she put it, "went haywire." I want to find and create pictures of myself and my children that document a life filled with love and self-nurturance—a life where we let our light shine.

– Claire, mom to Isabel, four, and Julio, two

final thoughts

If I were your fairy godmother and I could impart three qualities to support you on your journey to self-care, balance and living the life you desire, they would be:

Compassion for yourself. You are doing the very best you can wherever you are on your journey. Be easy on yourself, and remember, "good is good enough."

The ability to say "no" with ease. Become vigilant about how you manage your energy (not just your time); life is too short for you to spend time doing things that drain you.

A deep understanding of the transformative power of self-care. In making your self-care a priority, you will experience life as it was meant to be lived.

Turn to the *Guide* as your trusted friend and advocate. Read and re-read it. Do the exercises alone, with your family or ideally with a Personal Renewal Group. Realize that when you do, you're connecting with thousands of mothers who are reading or have read the *Guide* and experience many of the same feelings you do. Whether you are enjoying the *Guide* on your own or meeting with a Personal Renewal Group monthly to explore the themes/exercises, you are not alone. Reach out. Share from your heart— other women want meaningful connection and to be a part of a community, just like you do. Use the *Guide* as a catalyst for these conversations and gatherings. Let it change your life.

And be gentle with yourself.

I'd love to hear stories about how the *Guide* has impacted your life. Please email me at stories@reneetrudeau.com to share your experiences. And visit www.reneetrudeau.com for more information on *The Mother's Guide to Self-Renewal* and how to join or start a Personal Renewal Group in your community and for additional copies of the *Guide*.

I'll be thinking of you.

Warmly,
Renée

El Santuario de Chimayo, Chimayo, New Mexico

resources to support you

Get a Guide—Get a Group—Get Renewed!

Don't ask yourself what the world needs, ask yourself what makes you come alive. And then go do that. Because what the world needs are people who have come alive.

—Harold Whitman, professor/theologian

How to Start or Join a Personal Renewal Group (PRG) in Your Community

Below are some basic tips on how to start a PRG. You'll find more information and resources when you visit www.reneetrudeau.com.

- Good sources for recruiting potential PRG members are: playgroups, children's schools, existing moms' groups, entrepreneur groups, churches or spiritual communities, women's groups, yoga or meditation centers that offer programs for moms, military communities or bases, kid-centric programs (music classes, sports teams) and anywhere you'd find moms.

- To promote your new PRG, you may want to send out an email or post a flyer (make sure to mention that the group is based on the book, *The Mother's Guide to Self-Renewal*, and that they'll be asked to bring a copy to the first meeting). Ideally, promote the event at least six to eight weeks before your first meeting, if possible.

Olympic Peninsula, Washington State

Spring 2006 Personal Renewal Group, Austin, Texas: Rachel, Stephanie, Anne, Andrea, Claire, Teresa, Angela, Stralia, Bryna, Theresa, Misty, Cassandra, Laura, Karen, Bella and Wendy.

- The ideal group size is six to eight women, although you'll also find very powerful groups that are as small as three and as large as fifteen.*

- The ideal location for a group is a quiet, healing, private room or at someone's home (women often like sitting on the floor on pillows—each member can bring their own). You can often find free (or very low-cost) meeting space at libraries, hospitals, yoga studios, churches, schools or community centers.

- A good, realistic meeting schedule is to meet one night a month for two to three hours (e.g., the first Thursday night of each month from 7–9:30 p.m.). Set a schedule in advance so everyone can put the dates down on their calendar and arrange for child care.

- The *Guide* was created to be covered month by month during a complete calendar year. If you find it too hard to get people to commit to a year, you can offer a

For larger groups, it's highly recommended that the facilitator have previous experience leading support or coaching groups. Otherwise, this may feel a little overwhelming. See the end of this section for more information on becoming a trained PRG facilitator.

six-month session and then open enrollment to a second group for the second half of the year. Some groups may want to meet every two weeks for six months and cover all twelve chapters during a condensed period of time.

- You'll need one person to serve as the group facilitator. You can also rotate "hosts" each month and take turns leading the discussion and exercises, but it's really important that you have one person who is charged with keeping the group focused and on-track (otherwise it's very easy for the group dynamic to become purely social, and you miss out on the opportunity to delve into the themes and exercises). The group facilitator may choose to receive some training and resources through www.reneetrudeau.com.

- Set a group intention—what you want to get from the experience—when you first begin. For example, one intention I often use is that it's our goal that the PRG experience be nurturing, supportive and empowering. An intention is different from a goal as it often focuses on how you want to "be" as opposed to what you want to "do."

- Make sure you have plenty of time at the first meeting for individual introductions (name, age of children, why you were drawn to the PRG, etc.). It's good to build in lots of "get to know each other" time and exercises so the group members are comfortable with one another.

- Decide on ground rules or guidelines for the group (for example, you may ask that problem-solving and sharing of resources happen only during "break time" or before or after the meeting so you can make sure you cover all the material and stay focused). Or you may decide to all agree to maintain confidentiality about anything that is discussed at your PRG (this is highly recommended).

- I also recommend having each PRG member set individual intentions at the beginning of each PRG meeting. Create some quiet time when each member can pause and state this intention silently to herself before you begin.

- Make the group your own. Each month will have a theme, a story to illustrate the message, guided journaling and exercises to encourage members to put the theme into practice. Feel free to make up your own exercises or to skip some. Use the book as a guide for each month, but use your creativity to come up with specific ways to "play" with each monthly theme.

Coaches, counselors, parent educators and anyone else interested in working with and empowering mothers are invited to join the PRG Facilitators Community. You will receive online resources, ongoing support and tips to help you start, lead, promote and grow successful, powerful PRGs either as a component of your business or just for your own personal growth. Visit www.reneetrudeau.com to learn more.

To join an existing Personal Renewal Group, visit www.reneetrudeau.com and click on "Start/Join a Personal Renewal Group." Or, if you're starting a group and want to list your group meeting information on the site, email communities@reneetrudeau.com.

THE POWER OF SELF-CARE

The description for a Personal Renewal Group in my city came to me through a local listserv for mothers. My son was an infant, and I was exhausted, overwhelmed and suffering from that new-mother tunnel vision mindset in which you can only think about your next opportunity for sleep. So the phrases "reconnecting with who you are," "managing our energy" and "the transformative power of self-care" got my attention instantly. I thought the group organizer must have been a mind reader or an angel sent from heaven and I signed up. The group gave me so many things I desperately needed—a community of women, a community of mothers, nurturing and support, time for self-reflection and the opportunity to hear others' stories and share mine (validation). The chance to interact with other moms who were also interested in reconnecting with who they were before kids was really amazing.

—Cassandra, mom to Liam, age two

Community Building:
Getting Fed by Giving Back

You must be the change you
wish to see in the world.
—Mahatma Ghandi

In a world where people feel increasingly overworked, overscheduled and often isolated, I find the one thing that so many of us crave is a sense of connection and community.

Here are a few ideas on how you and your friends or your Personal Renewal Group can grow and nurture your sense of community:

● Consider having your PRG sponsor a "Mamas Helping Mamas" day. Sign your group members up to volunteer at a local shelter, a soup kitchen, a women's center, or another social service facility that supports families.

● Partner your PRG with a local social service agency that serves low-income mothers or teen mothers, and lead a mini one-day PRG workshop for these women. You can host this "Day of Renewal" at a local church, community center or the United Way and have a local restaurant donate lunch.

● Start quarterly or bimonthly PRG moms' night out events. You can tap into some of the exercises or themes in the book for inspiration on things to do. You might also encourage PRG fathers to start a dads' night out. Just being with friends is restorative and it reduces stress in our lives.

● Organize a "Day of Renewal" event for girls between the ages of eight and thirteen, teaching them in a fun and light-hearted way the importance of self-care and self love. Maybe even work with an existing organization to get this off the ground, such as the Girl Scouts.

● Start a meal co-op, babysitting co-op or household projects co-op (families rotate taking turns and helping each other tackle major household projects such as planting/landscaping, painting a house, cleaning out a garage, etc.) with your PRG or your friends. You can find out more details about how to set these up by searching the Internet.

- Start a "Big Girls Adventure Club." Each month one of the members of the Adventure Club is responsible for coming up with an idea for the group to try things they've never done before that may typically fall outside of their comfort zone. For example, the group might attend a local poetry reading, try rock climbing or take salsa classes.

- Host a neighborhood potluck for the families in your area. It's amazing how different you'll feel about your neighbors after you really take time to get to know them and their interests. Have everyone bring one clothing or household item to donate to a local social service agency.

- Check out New American Dream (a nonprofit dedicated to helping others live consciously, buy wisely and make a difference) at www.newdream.org. The site has some great articles, tips and resources on community building, particularly on nurturing our environment and teaching our kids the importance of doing so.

- Host a citywide garage sale with all the PRGs in your community and donate ten percent of the proceeds to a social service group that supports mothers and/or children.

- Visit artist Sara Hickman's nonprofit Web site (www.necessaryangels.org) to find out how to support, make a difference and get involved in helping others near and far.

Tips on Journaling

Writing is like making love. Don't worry about the orgasm, worry about the process.

—Isabel Allende

Are you new to journaling? Do you only write when you're feeling down or depressed? Not sure if you're doing it right?

Journaling is a powerful tool to help you process, release and tap into your feelings, desires and needs. It's also a great way to access your inner wisdom and gain clarity and focus on your life questions.

Here are some suggestions to help you feel more comfortable when journaling:

- Don't feel intimidated. Journaling isn't just for writers, it's for **everyone**.

- Release any preconceived ideas of what should or shouldn't be in your journal. A journal is as individual as the person writing in it.

- Your journal is for you and you alone. Let go of fears of judgment, dismiss the "shoulds" and let your thoughts and feelings flow out onto paper.

- Make yourself a cup of tea and curl up with paper and pen. Research shows that when we write in longhand, we're accessing both the left and right sides of our brain. When we're on the computer, it's much harder for us to fully utilize both of these hemispheres.

- Invest in yourself by taking the time to choose a special journal, either at a local bookstore, specialty paper store or online at a store like Running Rhino (www.runningrhino.com). Or just go buy a clean notebook from the grocery store. I like to have different journals for different periods of my life or creative projects. You might have your "career exploration journal" *and* your "releasing fears" journal, etc.

There is great power in putting thoughts on paper. Most people find journaling cathartic, healing and cleansing. Writing is a great way to explore your emotions and express what you're truly feeling.

Stuck on how to start? Try the "quickie journaling exercise": Write and answer the following three questions **every** morning for one week:

How do I feel?

What do I need?

What do I want?

It's a journal, not a novel. Don't feel that you have to write lengthy paragraphs; just "express" yourself and follow your gut on what feels right to you. Choose one word, jot down phrases or ideas or even sketch your thoughts.

If you're worried about others reading what you wrote, feel free to write and then burn or shred those pages from your journal. You'll still get the full benefit of the journaling experience.

Make the time to journal. Set aside regular journaling dates—daily would be ideal, but weekly is just fine. Create a cozy space for journaling and make it as comfortable and inviting as possible—with a special chair or floor pillow, your favorite blanket or tea. Go to the same space each time you journal.

Decide what time of the day you like to journal. Many people say they are freshest first thing in the morning, while others like to journal at night before bed. Some find it releases the stress of the day.

Like anything, journal writing takes practice and patience. Keep at it, even if you just write a few lines a week.

Visit www.journalution.com, a great resource with a monthly newsletter that offers journaling tips and prompts for journaling. Sandy Grason's book, *Journalution* is also highly recommended.

Resources for Mothers Managing Depression

This special section is dedicated to the gentle, caring spirit of 2006 Austin PRG member Michelle Boeckman, mom to Taylor. May her light shine always.

> Without emotion, man would be nothing but a biological computer. Love, joy, sorrow, fear, apprehension, anger, satisfaction, and discontent provide the meaning of human existence.
>
> —Arnold M. Ludwig, psychologist

If you find yourself having extremely negative reactions as you read the *Guide*, such as feelings of hopelessness, intense self-criticism or exhaustion, these could possibly be signs of depression. Be gentle with yourself and talk about your feelings with a friend, a counselor, your ob-gyn or midwife or your family doctor.

The rate of depression among women with small children is extremely high. If you know you are predisposed to and/or suffer from depression, please know that you are not alone and that there are many avenues for help.

Below are some recommended resources to support you:

BOOKS

Down Came the Rain: My Journey Through Postpartum Depression, by Brooke Shields

Inconsolable: How I Threw My Mental Health Out with the Diapers, by Marrit Ingman

THERAPIST REFERRAL RESOURCES

American Group Psychotherapy Association

www.agpa.org

Find a certified group therapist on this national Web site (a great resource for women who need help and want to connect with other women).

American Psychological Association

www.apa.org

Click on the Find a Psychologist link on the home page to view a partial list of licensed psychologists.

Imago Therapy

www.imagorelationships.org

Find an Imago therapist and learn more about a leading approach to enhancing couples' communication skills and strengthening marriages.

WEB SITES

Postpartum Support International
www.postpartum.net
Includes information on support groups in your area

Postpartum Education for Parents
www.sbpep.org/index.php
*Education and resources for parents, including a "warm line"
you can call with questions*

Depression and Bipolar Support Alliance
www.dbsalliance.org
Includes information on groups in your area

Postpartum screening quiz
pregnancy.about.com/od/postpartumdepress/a/ppdquiz.htm

A depression screening test
www.depression-screening.org

The Online PPD Support Group
www.ppdsupportpage.com

Centre for Suicide Prevention (Canada)
www.suicideinfo.ca

Suicide Prevention Action Network USA (SPAN USA)
www.spanusa.org

Kristin Brooks Hope Center (KBHC) and National Hopeline Network
www.hopeline.com

Renée Peterson Trudeau

Raised by an artist/healer/teacher/musician mother and physician father, Renée is the oldest of seven children.

Born in 1966 in Houston, Texas, she grew up in San Antonio, where she attended Montessori school, and the Sierra Nevada Mountains of Northern California, where she attended a Waldorf-based yoga school and rode horses, hiked in the deep snow near the Donner Pass and learned stained glass window making and philosophy from the Bhagavad-Gita.

Renée's parents were "truth seekers" from as far back as she can remember—this is clearly evidenced by her siblings' names, which range from Teresa to Shiva. Their spiritual quest had a huge impact on her upbringing and sense of self.

In the 1990s, Renée tragically and unexpectedly lost her nineteen-year-old brother to suicide and her father to a heart attack. Her mother passed suddenly from congestive heart failure in 2000.

These losses had a profound impact on Renée's life and career path, and left her with a sense of urgency and desire to help others find and express their life purpose and live the life they desire. The deaths also impressed upon her the importance of community and connection with others.

Today, Renée is a career and work/life balance coach and president of Austin-based Career Strategists, a nationally-recognized career coaching/consulting firm dedicated to helping professionals and entrepreneurs integrate *who they are* with *what they do.*

She has helped thousands of professionals throughout the United States to strategically manage their careers while maximizing job satisfaction, learn how to create and promote their personal brands, put together plans for career change, develop and launch small businesses that support their life goals and invent ways to balance work and family that energize rather than drain them.

Her clients include professionals employed by IBM, Shell Oil, Whole Foods Market, 3M, GSD&M Advertising, AMD, State Farm Insurance, MCI, Amazon.com, Dell Computer Corporation, Accenture, Freescale, National Instruments, Samsung and state and federal government agencies and nonprofit organizations.

Additionally, she leads work/life balance workshops for Fortune 500 companies and professional organizations such as Women in Technology, EWomen Network and Executive Women in Government.

Her unique approach to career management has been featured in numerous publications, including *Working Mother*, *Family Circle*, *Parenting*, *Pregnancy* and *American Way* and in numerous broadcast, print and online business media.

Renée lives in Austin, Texas with her husband and son.

For more information, visit www.reneetrudeau.com.

acknowledgments

Any great creative project that sets out to touch millions of lives is the collective work of many. From the deepest place in my heart, I thank my unbelievable Renewal Team: Bella Guzmán, Rachel Hobson, Anne Hebert, Amy Hufford, Wendy Morgan, Laura Bond Williams, Linden Kohtz and Lisa Sandeford for their amazing efforts and undying support for the book project. The *Guide* would not be in your hands were it not for these very special, generous women and their hard work.

To the hundreds of courageous mothers who have participated in my Austin-based Personal Renewal Groups since 2002. You are my teachers and my inspiration for this project; your sharing and vulnerability continue to touch my life in so many ways.

To the amazing women in my Yogamamas playgroup. Our conversations on the playground and over kid dinners have nourished me in more ways than you'll ever know.

To the supportive, loving, creative and amazing friends I've met through the Primavera Montessori School Community, truly one of the places my family calls home.

To my "wise women" mentor friends: Margaret Keys, Gail Allen, Joyce Lyle, Patti Halladay, Jill Carey, Nelin Hudani, Frances Cox and Celeste Hamman. Your support is always felt, even if it's just through the ethers. Thank you for all you do for me.

To the inspiring, innovative and business-savvy women in my Business + Balance Success Group and in the Austin Chapter of the Association for Women in Communications, two groups that continually support me and feed me, no matter where I am on my career or life path.

To the hard-working, book-publishing marketing minds of Cyndi Hughes, Marika Flatt, Jennifer Hill Robenalt, George Sutton and Cheri Lomonte. Thank you for your time, ideas, encouragement and belief in me and my project.

To my wonderful colleagues at the Austin Chapter of the International Coaches Federation. Your dedication to personal transformation inspires and motivates me to keep innovating new ways to serve and support others.

To fellow authors/coaches, Martha Beck, Cheryl Richardson and Debbie Ford, thank you for paving the path, lighting the way and sharing your voices and hearts with the world. We are fortunate to have such amazing catalysts for personal growth in our midst.

To my amazing grandmothers, Mabel Harrison and Marie Peterson, thank you for instilling in me strength and individuality.

To my endlessly fascinating siblings: Kert, Sean, Nathan, Timothy and Teresa. Their smarts, creativity and inquisitive natures remind me to keep asking the questions.

To Career Strategists and my amazing career coaching clients—thank you for the opportunity to serve you and for all you have taught me. Supporting you has been a privilege. And also to Balanced Living Press; your presence has been key to this project's success! Thank you for helping me help others.

To John, the most supportive, grounding and wise man I know. Thank you for your love, guidance and patience and for being my life partner. The labor was long, but the baby has arrived!

To Jonah, the brightest light in my life and my soul's inspiration for helping mothers create the life they desire. It is a privilege to be your mother, and I am honored to be your pupil.

To God, my source for all the good that flows to and from me. I am grateful to be of service. Thank you for your guidance on this project and in all that I do.

To my parents, Kit and Julie Peterson.
Your generosity, authenticity, passion, creativity
and drive for excellence amazed and continues
to inspire me. Thank you for opening my heart,
fueling my creativity, encouraging my innovation,
challenging my intellect, expanding my concept
of God and spirituality and constantly encouraging
me to question who I am and what I'm here to do.
I am grateful to have had you as teachers.

Juliana Harrison Peterson (1939–2000) and
Frances "Kit" Peterson, MD (1940–1996),
parents to Renée, Kert, Geoffrey (1971–1992),
Shiva Sean, Nathan, Timothy and Teresa.

How to Order Additional Copies of the Guide

To order additional copies of *The Mother's Guide to Self-Renewal: How to Reclaim, Rejuvenate and Re-Balance Your Life*, visit our Web site at www.reneetrudeau.com. Bulk discounts are available for group purchases.

HOW TO CONTACT US

For ongoing support, visit www.reneetrudeau.com to find the following:

- Additional information on how to start a Personal Renewal Group (PRG) for mothers.

- Information on joining an existing PRG in your community.

- Information on training, certification programs and resources for PRG facilitators.

- Recommended resources to support your personal growth and self-care practice.

- How to join our community and subscribe to our online Renewal Newsletter.

- How to purchase books for your Personal Renewal Group at a bulk discount.

- How to contact Renée Trudeau regarding her availability for a private workshop, training seminar or keynote address.

Write or email us at:

Renée Trudeau & Associates
4107 Medical Parkway, Suite 104
Austin, TX 78756
info@reneetrudeau.com
www.reneetrudeau.com